WITHDRAWN STACKS

We Were Vagabonds

Sequel to Father Was A Caveman

June Harman Betts

authorHOUSE®

AuthorHouse™
1663 Liberty Drive, Suite 200
Bloomington, IN 47403
www.authorhouse.com
Phone: 1-800-839-8640

© 2009 June Harman Betts. All rights reserved.

No part of this book may be reproduced, stored in a retrieval system, or transmitted by any means without the written permission of the author.

First published by AuthorHouse   1/10/2009

ISBN: 978-1-4343-6876-8 (sc)
ISBN: 978-1-4389-3373-3 (hc)

Printed in the United States of America
Bloomington, Indiana

This book is printed on acid-free paper.

Books by June Harman Betts

Echoes In My Mind Series

    Book 1: Father Was A Caveman
    Book 2: We Were Vagabonds
    Book 3: Along Came A Soldier - *Coming in early 2009!*

The following is a brief summary of Father Was A Caveman, the first book in the Echoes In My Mind Series:

FATHER WAS A CAVEMAN, ABBREVIATED

Life was like a Shirley Temple movie, upbeat and carefree.
Life was like a backyard swing, uplifting and happy.
Life was like an open field, adventurous and inviting.
Life was like a carrousel in your front yard, fun and exciting.
Life was like a whipped cream pie, sweet and fulfilling.
Life was like hugs and kisses from Mom and Dad, loving and willing.

THEN ALL WAS PIERCED BY GUNSHOTS, INJURED BY ILLNESS, AND SHATTERED BY STRANGERS!

Gone was the backyard swing,
    open field panoramas,
        Mom's hugs and kisses,
            and the promise of Shirley Temple pajamas.

Then life was like a dreary house, dark and refused.
Life was like a lonely child, sad and confused.
Life was like a mean uncle, threatening and overbearing.
Life was like the town gossips, hurtful and uncaring.

Suddenly out of the blue
There came a young woman to the rescue.
She offered a second chance.
Life once again became a joyous dance.
Her open heart brought back the sun.
The Lone Ranger and Scarlett O'Hara wrapped in one.

        Written by Janice Large
        Dedicated to her Mom,
          June Harman Betts
       And MaMa Polly Harman

ACKNOWLEDGEMENTS

I want to thank Janice Large, my editor, my indispensable partner for the many hours she spent working with me on the editing and also for her helpful suggestions and valuable assistance; Ric Betz for capturing the essence of the story in his interior illustrations; and Mike and Eric Large for their patient and unending technical assistance.

The Vagabond Years

FLASHBACK!
HOW THEY BECAME A FAMILY OF FOUR

"Christmas is almost here, and you still haven't told me what you want. These last few months that I've known you have been great, and I really want to get you something special," Burrel told the redheaded woman walking beside him.

"Oh, so you were just pretending that you wanted to go for a walk on a snowy Christmas Eve in Baltimore when what you really wanted was to get me to point something out to you in this store window," she teased when she realized he had maneuvered her to the front of a small jewelry store and was peering in the window.

"Guilty as charged," he retorted. "If you would rather, we could go down the street to one of the department stores and check out some of those frilly things women like to wear."

As the last word escaped his mouth, she wasn't sure whether he was blushing or if his checks were red from the frigid air. Reaching up, she brushed the snow flakes from his dark blond hair before she softly said, "If I could have anything I want for Christmas, it would be to have your children."

He questioned his hearing as her words echoed in his mind. "Did you just say that you want to have children by me? I know this is 1941 and you are a modern woman but if I had suggested such a thing, you would have slapped my face!"

Caught between amusement and anger she suggested they slip around the corner so they could talk at the small restaurant they often frequented. Once they settled into a booth and ordered coffee, he took up where he'd left off, "You know I love you, but this isn't the time for me to have more children since I'm separated from the ones I have. I haven't been able to keep them with me since their mother took our youngest son and left me and the two older children almost a year ago. You know that they are living with my sisters in West Virginia, but if I could have anything I wanted for Christmas this year, it would be to be able to make a home where we can be together. Do you think a guardian angel is going to show up and make it happen?"

Tears were forming in her eyes as he spoke, but before she could respond, the waitress sat the hot steaming coffee in front of them. Polly watched Burrel stir four teaspoons of sugar and a hearty amount of cream into his coffee before she sipped hers and said, "I've never been accused of being a guardian angel but that is exactly what I am suggesting. I didn't mean that I wanted to have a baby, at least not yet. I meant that I want to take you up on your offer to share your life with you and your children. I want to raise June and Cecil, alongside you. I want them with us when you start your new job in Zanesville, Ohio." Then hesitantly she murmured, "I think your children like me."

He interrupted to say, "Like you? They love you! June has already told me she wants you to be her mother. Cecil hasn't said, but I think he feels the same way. That would be a great Christmas present for all of us. The kids would love to be a family again."

He drained his cup and stood up before he suggested that they go back to the jewelry store. While he was helping her into her new camel hair coat, his eyes twinkled when he grinned and said, "I'm not sure who did the proposing here."

She returned his grin and quipped, "After weeks of you fishing for an answer, I finally took the bait, so you're the one who proposed. I just accepted."

"You do understand what I am offering, don't you?" At her affirmative nod, their eyes locked in understanding and he declared, "I have never loved you more than I do at this moment. Now let's go and get you a ring. I was going to pick one out, but I thought, since this was something you would be wearing the rest of your life, you might want to choose it yourself."

She smiled and said, "I'm glad you didn't buy a diamond for me as I really don't like them. I've always wanted a pearl ring."

When they stepped inside the brightly lit store they were met by the strains of, Oh, Holy Night. Burrel felt that on this particular Holy Night, his future was looking good, thanks to the redheaded angel standing next to him.

He wondered since she was only twenty-two, if she might be taking on more than she would be able to handle. Later after they were together as a family, though, Polly and the children's antics would keep him on his toes and he sometimes would wonder what he had gotten himself into that snowy night in Baltimore.

CHAPTER ONE

FAMILY OF FOUR

June opened her eyes to the winter sunlight streaming in through the windows. As she had every morning since she had arrived at the house on Taylor Street, she marveled at the new direction her life had taken.

After a difficult year, of being scattered apart, her father had given her the best Christmas gift ever, the miracle of being a family again. As this thought crossed her mind, she felt a momentary twinge of sadness at the thought that it wasn't the original family of five she'd had, but her spirits lifted at the thought of this new family. After being separated, they were now reunited and blessed with this delightful new mother. It was hard to believe they had only been together for a few weeks.

Her thoughts were interrupted by the sound of a soft southern voice calling up the steps to inform them that breakfast would be ready in a few minutes. Moments later, when she entered the dining room, her father, brother and her new mother, the source of the soft southern voice, were seated at the table.

While they ate, she openly admired this young redheaded woman, and marveled at the fact that at twenty-two years of age, she hadn't batted an eye at the thought that if she married Burrel, his thirteen-year-old son and eleven-year-old daughter would be part of the package.

While people they had met since they moved to Zanesville were surprised at the youth of the mother, no one suspected that they hadn't always been a family. The fact that they had called her "Mom" from the first moment helped.

~

When they finished breakfast June and Cecil went outside to build a snowman, and Burrel and Polly remained talking at the table while having a second cup of coffee. After laughing at one of Polly's comments, Burrel said, "Sometimes you say the funniest things, but the funniest was when I asked you what you wanted for Christmas and you blurted out, 'I want to have your children!'"

Polly quickly responded, "I can't believe you thought I wanted to have a baby! I thought you knew that I loved your children as much as I loved you."

She refilled their cups before she flippantly quipped, "I got the best of the deal. I got the three of you and all you got was me." Then wiggling the third finger of her left hand she said, "Besides that I got this lovely pearl ring."

Burrel responded, "I think you are the first woman I've ever met who doesn't like diamonds." He chuckled before seriously adding, "I think I came out pretty well on this deal. I got you."

She leaned across the table and planted a kiss on his lips before she saucily replied, "Then we both hit the jackpot!"

~

Their new home on Taylor Street in Zanesville was a two story yellow frame one, located two houses off Maple Avenue, a main thoroughfare. The living room, with an open stairway at one end, stretched across the width of the house. Making up the rest of the downstairs was a dining room, kitchen, pantry, and a landing which led to the basement. There were three rooms and a bath on the second floor.

Since they had so little furniture, the rooms seemed cavernous. June and Cecil loved the space, but Polly liked small cozy places. She never quite got used to the size of the house on Taylor Street.

She and Burrel had managed to scrape together enough money to buy a minimal amount of furniture which consisted of a white iron double bed and wooden dresser for each of the three bedrooms, dining room table and chairs for the dining room, a used couch, and a couple of upholstered chairs for the living room.

That night as they sat in the living room around the radio listening to The Shadow, they were all four immersed in the mystery. At the end, Cecil blurted out, "But the police never arrested the man who shot you, did they, Dad?" They all knew he was referring to the shooter who had bushwhacked Burrel a few years earlier when they were living at the cavern house in West Virginia.

Thinking of the shotgun pellets that were left near his brain, Burrel answered, "No Son, that man got away with attempted murder. If I'd been any closer to where he was hiding when I walked from the house that night to check the animals, the shotgun blast would have killed me." Burrel sighed and mused, "All that because I dismissed him from his job at the cavern."

Polly interjected, "He may have gotten away with it on earth, but he'll have to answer to his Maker someday!"

June shuttered at the memory of seeing her father stumble through the door after being shot, and all the bright red blood that was seeping through his white shirt and pants.

Pumped up by all the talk of guns, Cecil asked, "Hey, Mom, did Dad ever tell you about the time our crazed neighbor woman held a shotgun on June, Dickie, and I when we were on our way to our mailbox?"

Polly briskly replied, "Oh yes, and I am certainly thankful your mother got her calmed down before the gun went off and anyone was hurt. Enough talk of guns. Let's listen to something less violent before we go to bed or we'll all have nightmares. How about listening to Amos and Andy?"

After all they'd been hearing on the news about the war with Germany and Japan since Japan bombed Pearl Harbor less than a month earlier they were ready for some light entertainment.

Later as they were preparing for bed, Polly told Burrel, "I didn't want to mention it in front of the kids, but today I received a letter from the Baltimore police. They say that they feel I am safe from any more threats from Tony Torintino after their very strong warnings of deportation back to Argentina."

Burrel agreed, "The police very forcefully got their point across to him."

Polly pondered, "I'll never forget the night Tony came into Hashslingers Restaurant at the end of my shift and tried to kidnap me. When I saw he had a gun, I was petrified. I barely escaped out of that bathroom window. If I'd weighed a pound more, I wouldn't have been able to squeeze through. You'll never know how relieved I was to see you there waiting for me in your car." She smiled flirtatiously before she added, "You were certainly my knight in shining armor that night."

Burrel bowed, and said, "At your service anytime, My Lady." She threw her arms around him and gave him a big hug before they tumbled over onto their bed.

The next morning, Polly woke gently after having a peaceful dream of her parents' home in Mississippi. It had seemed so real, that she could actually feel the hot southern breeze warm her body. As she opened her eyes, she saw the snow outside and realized that she was up North, not down South.

Occupying space in the basement was a large object she hated with a passion. It was a cast iron furnace that constantly needed to be fueled. Consuming bucket after bucket of coal, in return it cast off mounds of ashes that needed to be emptied.

Since Burrel, Cecil, and June's schedules kept them away from home for hours at a time, Polly soon became the reluctant keeper of the flames.

"That big black monster" was the mildest of the epithets she bestowed upon it as she struggled with keeping a fire going. Having grown up in the South, this was a new experience for her, one she readily turned over to Burrel and Cecil when they were home.

Another chore she disliked, almost as much, was the laundry. When they'd been shopping for furniture, there hadn't been money for a washing machine. Polly, being young and inexperienced as a housewife, had bravely stated, "I don't need a washing machine. I'll just wash them in the bathtub."

It didn't take her long to learn the folly of those words and to find a convenient laundry where the dirty clothes could be dropped off and picked up a few days later, fresh and clean, ready to be ironed. She was proud of herself. She'd not only discovered the best work saver for women since store bought bread, but also found a way to finance it and still be at home for the children.

She had gotten the idea when she'd heard Burrel's brother-in-law, Verde, and a West Virginia neighbor, Don Bland, co-workers at the plant, complain about growing tired of restaurant food.

"I've been trying to think of a way I can earn some money," she told Burrel one morning while they were sitting at the breakfast table lingering over their second cup of coffee. "Do you think Verde and Don would be interested in eating here? I could cook dinner for them and prepare their lunches five days a week. I could probably do it for less than they pay in a restaurant. Besides, what I cook would taste much better."

At first, Burrel was reluctant to accept her suggestion. He felt it wasn't right to charge his brother-in-law and friend, but after some discussion, he agreed to broach the subject with Verde, and if he thought it was a good idea, he'd talk to Don.

Polly wasn't surprised to find they'd both jumped at the chance to eat home cooked food in a real home. She soon found herself, not only able to pay the laundry bill, but also to buy June and Cecil some much needed clothes. With one look at the hems of their coats barely skimming their thighs, she had no trouble deciding on their first shopping trip where the money was to go.

June's new coat was reversible with one side plain beige and the other a blue and beige plaid. Cecil's was a blue plaid wool mackintosh. Standing back and surveying them, in their new finery she said, "I'd say you both look pretty groovy! Now all we have to do is get June that permanent she's always wanted and Cece a haircut, and you'll be all set."

"A permanent! Am I really getting a permanent?" June asked.

"I like your hair the way it is, but since you have your heart set on curly hair, how can I refuse?" Polly replied.

When June emerged from the beauty shop, her swinging, shiny straight hair replaced by such a mass of curls it would have been difficult getting it into a bushel basket, Polly's first thought was, "Good heavens! I'm going to have to learn to say no!"

∼

When the holidays were over and it was time for them to go to school, they had managed to tame June's wild locks. Ready for their first day, they looked nice in their new finery, June in the dress Polly had made for her and Cece in a new bright blue sweater and corduroy trousers.

As they set off for the bus, with their new coats buttoned to their chins, Polly gave them each a big hug and said, "Go get them, Tigers!"

That first day the entire city was blanketed with snow. While it was beautiful to look at they didn't enjoy being out in it. As they waited for the bus, the wind accompanying the snow soon turned their cheeks and noses a vivid red. Turning up their collars, they were thankful for their new winter coats.

Roosevelt Junior High School was the first of many schools June and Cecil would be attending in the next few years, schools where they found themselves in a room full of strangers. They were never to forget, or get used to the experience of standing in front of the room with every eye on them as they were introduced to the class. Even though they had changed schools many times, always before they'd known someone in the class, either friends they'd made before school started or, as often had been the case, their cousins.

To their surprise, they managed to get through the day without getting lost. Polly was anxiously waiting at the door, eager to hear all about their first day. "Okay, tell me about it. How did you get along?" she asked.

"It was really different," June said, "We change rooms for each class. I probably would have gotten lost, but a girl in my homeroom asked me to walk along with her. You should have seen everyone rushing through the halls."

"Yeah," Cecil said, "If you didn't keep on moving, you'd have been run over."

"They show a movie during the lunch period!" June exclaimed.

"A movie?" Polly asked. "That must have been a long lunch period!"

"They don't show a whole movie. A boy I ate with said they show a little bit of the movie each day. It takes all week to see the whole thing. This week we're seeing Gunga Din. It's pretty exciting!"

"That's a good movie," Polly said. "I saw that in New Orleans when I was in nurse's training." Then smiling at June, she added, "I bet I know what June liked."

"Yeah, what?" June asked.

"Cary Grant! I bet all the girls liked him. He's not bad to look at."

"Not bad at all," June sighed.

Having heard enough, Cecil exclaimed, "Yuk! Mushy stuff," as he picked up his books and headed for his room.

∼

The first few weeks in their new home, Burrel was working overtime. Polly, June, and Cecil took advantage of the time to get better acquainted. Though they had started calling her Mom, she seemed more like a not too much older sister.

Saturdays they would play in the snow, making a snowman or having a battle with snowballs. The rare time when the ground was free of snow, they decided to teach their new mother how to ride a bicycle.

The blond girl and boy soon became a familiar sight on Taylor and Maple Avenue, as one on each side, they walked along supporting their red-headed mother who was seated on the bicycle trying unsuccessfully to maintain her balance.

June told Polly, "Cecil and I had the same problem when Tony and Pauline taught us to ride. We got the hang of it though and you will too."

At her daughter's words, Polly put her feet down and stopped the lesson for a moment as she explosively proclaimed, "Your dad's nudist spelunker friend taught you two to ride a bike!" She couldn't contain a giggle at the picture her imagination conveyed of a nude man on one side and his nude wife on the other guiding the student rider down the streets of Arlington. "Did they at least wear shoes?" she asked between giggles.

"Aw, Mom." June replied. "They wore clothes when they were outside. When we were inside, Tony only wore his shoes, socks, and glasses."

Her amusement faded as she fervently exclaimed, "Around the two of you!" Then torn between amusement and concern, she added, "I'm not sure I like hearing that!"

Cecil replied, "It was okay, Mom. Dad had explained to us before we spent a couple weeks with them that Tony had told him when the two of them were exploring the cavern that he and Pauline were nudists. I guess at first Dad was shocked by it, but he wouldn't have let us visit them if he didn't think Tony was okay."

"June and I were a little shocked when Tony first walked into the living room in his birthday suit, but he acted like going without clothes was the most natural thing in the world. We didn't mind him doing it, but we certainly weren't going to take ours off!"

He positioned himself on one side of the bike and signaled for his sister to get back on her side before he said, "Now let's get back to your lesson."

Polly reluctantly put her feet back on the pedals, and valiantly tried to ride for a few feet. "This blasted thing has a mind of its own!" she cried, as she veered off toward the street. The only thing that kept her from falling was the support of the sturdy young arms of her children.

"Mom, you have to sit up straight! Quit leaning to the side!" Cecil ordered.

As she wove from one side of the sidewalk to the other, Polly exclaimed, "I'm trying! I'm trying! Give me a little time and I'll learn." Any thought she'd had that they were going to let her give up was belied by the look she saw them exchange. "I might as well learn," she thought, "or they'll never let me off this blasted machine."

"I've never experienced such terror," she told Burrel that night while they were lying in bed. "I was sure I was going to fall off and break my neck."

Nuzzling close to her, he said, "That's such a nice neck. I wouldn't want to have anything happen to it." Then in a more serious vein, he added, "You don't have to do it. Just tell them you've changed your mind."

"I can't do that," she emphatically stated. "What kind of an example would that be? I want these kids to know they can do anything they set out to do. How would it look if I gave up on this thing?"

Using his most soothing tone, Burrel murmured, "Calm down. It was just a suggestion. I hadn't really thought about it, but I can see your point."

Frightened though she was, she did finally learn, and in so doing taught her teachers a lesson in courage and perseverance they never forgot.

～

They all loved movies, so Saturday matinee found them sitting in the dark, watching the action on the silver screen. Polly's favorite movie stars were the singers Jeanette McDonald and Nelson Eddy. Over the years, she saw to it they never missed one of their movies.

That year of 1942, the latest movies came to downtown Zanesville. Some made them laugh, while others made the females cry. Some were classics, like How Green Was My Valley, while the majority were merely entertaining.

After taking them to see Honky Tonk, starring Clark Gable and Lana Turner, two of Hollywood's most famous stars, Polly told them Honky Tonk was another word for a bar. When their dad got home that evening she was going to tease him by saying they'd spent the afternoon at a Honky Tonk. "Now, go along with me," she said. "We should really get him going before we tell him that was the name of the movie."

They'd never played a joke on their dad before, but Polly was having so much fun at the prospect of his reaction, that they didn't want to spoil it for her.

Their little joke fell through, though, as Burrel had never heard of a bar being called a Honky Tonk, and he had no idea what she was talking about.

He looked so puzzled, they found themselves laughing and feeling more than a little foolish. When they explained what they'd been up to, he just shook his head. This young woman and his children made quite a team. Not for the first time, he marveled at her youth.

～

June and Irvalee Schenk, the dark haired girl who had befriended her the first day of school, soon became friends. Many evenings after school, the girls visited in each other's homes. One evening as Polly overheard them talking, Irvalee was saying, "Your mother doesn't look old enough to have kids as old as you and Cecil."

Though June had heard her, she didn't reply. It was still painful for her to say that her parents were divorced. She was proud of her new Mom and their new family, but this didn't keep her from feeling that if she uttered the words, "My parents are divorced. This is my stepmother," she would be letting her mother, Priscilla, go. This time it would be forever.

Thinking her friend hadn't heard her, Irvalee repeated her statement. Polly looked first at one girl, then the other. Seeing June's dilemma, she spoke up, "Thanks for the compliment! It's always nice to hear someone say that I look young!"

"You do!" Irvalee insisted. "I have a sister who's twenty! You don't look any older than she does."

Laughing, Polly truthfully replied, "I'm certainly older than twenty." The look she and June exchanged, though, said plainer than words, "How much older, will be our little secret."

This episode made her more than ever conscious that people weren't taking her seriously as June and Cecil's mother. With this realization, she was determined to do something to make herself look the part.

Sitting in front of the vanity mirror in her bedroom later that afternoon, she parted her hair down the middle and tightly pulled it away from her face. Studying the results in the mirror she muttered, "That's better." Then with nimble fingers she plaited it into two braids, wrapped them severely around her head and fastened them firmly in place with bobby pins.

Examining her handiwork in the mirror, she still wasn't quite satisfied. "It's the makeup," she thought. Grabbing a tissue and some cleansing cream, she quickly removed her carefully applied foundation, powder, and mascara. Last to go was her usual splash of bright red lipstick. "That'll do it," she said, as she took one last look in the mirror before going downstairs to prepare dinner.

The expression on Burrel's face when he walked into the kitchen was pure amazement. "What have you done to yourself?" he exclaimed. "Or should I ask, where's Polly?"

Surprised at his reaction, she was almost at a loss for words as she stammered, "I thought I should look older, so people would think I was June and Cecil's mother."

"Mother! Good heavens, Woman, they'll think you're their grandmother! If I'd wanted an old woman I expect I could have found one," he said.

"All I can say is, if you set out to make yourself look older, you certainly succeeded." Then turning to June and Cecil, who had been quietly listening, he said, "Is this what you want your Mom to look like?"

They'd been as stunned as he was at the transformation, but hadn't known what to say. Now that their father had brought up the subject, they were quick to say they liked her better the other way.

"I love the way you've always worn your hair," June said. Having spent months being exposed to gossip about her family, she wasn't about to care whether people thought Polly was too young to be her mother. She, Cecil, and their dad liked her the way she was, and, to her, that was all that mattered.

The next evening, when June and Cecil got home from school and Burrel from work, they were pleased and relieved to again find her looking young and pretty.

"That's my girl!" Burrel said. Then turning to June and Cecil, he asked, "Don't you think your Mom looks prettier with her hair this way?"

Seeing them nod in agreement, she looked contrite as she replied, "You've made your point. I'll never try that again."

A smile that had been twitching at the corners of his mouth spread until he was grinning from ear to ear. Then no longer able to contain it, roars of laughter poured from his throat. "That's the funniest thing you've ever done. I almost didn't recognize you!" he said.

Looking as if she didn't know whether to laugh or cry, she finally stammered, "I didn't think it was that funny."

Pulling her onto his lap, he said, "Come on now. Admit it. It was funny."

Seeing the tears of laughter streaming down his cheeks and feeling his arms around her, she couldn't stay angry. Instead she found herself joining in the laughter. "You haven't met Mamma yet," she said. "That's the way she wears her hair."

Burrel asked, "How old is your Mamma?"

"I guess she's around sixty-five," she replied.

This brought on more laughter as Burrel said, "You wanted to look sixty-five? That would make you old enough to be my mother!" While this banter continued, June and Cecil decided to go into the living room and listen to the radio. It looked like their mom and dad had forgotten all about dinner.

The time spent in Zanesville was filled with happiness and laughter. It was almost as if they were trying to make up for the sadness of the previous months.

"It's time for Sleepy Head to get out of bed and celebrate!" were the first words June heard the morning of January twenty-fifth, her twelfth birthday. "Come on, June. Don't you want to see your presents?" Polly asked.

Rubbing the sleep from her eyes, she jumped out of bed and ran down the hall to her parents' room. Standing outside their door, she called out, "Where are my presents?"

Hearing Polly say, "Come on in," she entered the room, to find her dad, Cecil and Polly sitting on the bed, surrounded by colorfully wrapped packages.

As June stared, Polly exclaimed, "What are you waiting for? Come on. Open them!"

Patting a place on the bed, Burrel moved over, making room for her to sit next to him. "Here, open mine first," Cecil said, as he handed one to her. Sitting between her dad and mom, her eyes shining, she carefully removed the ribbon and paper and opened the box.

Nestled in layers of tissues was a pair of orange colored pajamas. As she removed them from their wrapping, a momentary look of sadness crossed her face. She was remembering the promise her mother, Priscilla, had made before leaving her at her aunt's. She had said that when she returned, she would bring her a present, a pair of Shirley Temple style satin pajamas. But then, she had never returned.

Noticing June's expression, Polly asked, "What's the matter, June Baby? Don't you like them?"

"I love them," she replied. "Thank you. They're beautiful."

Opening the next present brought a squeal of delight. "A robe! It's what I've always wanted." As she wrapped the long, quilted, paisley printed garment around her, she continued to exclaim, "It's orange. I've always loved orange! It matches my new pajamas."

This birthday marked the beginning of a new family tradition. The birthday person was pampered, getting to choose the menu for the day. Polly wasn't sure what combinations might be requested, but she found June's order easy to fill. She wanted Polly's special scrambled eggs, toast with jelly for breakfast, and ham, pineapple, ambrosia and sweet potatoes covered with melted marshmallows for dinner. The last two were among the many traditional southern recipes Polly had brought with her. June loved the taste of the different kinds of food Polly prepared. Burrel occasionally grumbled, though, because he missed his West Virginia style homemade biscuits, milk gravy, and fried potatoes. Although her taste was more sophisticated, Polly made up her mind she was going to learn to cook his favorite dishes. Her first attempts to make the gravy were disastrous. Though it tasted more like library paste than gravy, they didn't want to hurt her feelings, so they forced it down.

After they'd almost resigned themselves to this state of affairs, she finally succeeded. One evening at dinner, the food was excellent. The gravy was smooth and creamy, the potatoes fried to perfection, and the biscuits light as a feather.

From then on their meals were unique, a mixture of both their tastes. This, with the other traditions they were developing, and the love they all felt for each other, began the process of bonding them together as a strong family unit.

~

This new family of Polly's constantly challenged her. She hardly had time to bask in their compliments for her newly developed culinary skills, when Cecil presented her with another problem.

One Friday night, Roosevelt Junior High School was having a dance for the ninth graders. Cecil and a few of his classmates were going together. That evening, when he nonchalantly strolled downstairs, he looked handsome in his dress slacks, white shirt, and V necked sweater. Handing his necktie to Polly he asked, "How do you tie one of these?"

She stared at it as if expecting it to bite her. "I haven't the least idea," she said. "Your dad will be home soon. He can tie it for you."

"But Mom," Cecil exclaimed, "The kids will be here in a few minutes. Can't you do it?"

"I'll try," she said. She had realized weeks before, that June and Cecil thought she could do everything. "I'm afraid," she thought, "this is going to be the time they find out how wrong they are."

Standing facing Cecil, she remembered watching Burrel place a tie around his neck and with a few flicks of the hand produce a perfect Windsor knot. "I think, this is the way he did it," she said, looping it around his neck. "I think he went right over left and left over right. When I pull on this end, that should do it."

Standing back, surveying her handiwork, she could hardly believe her eyes. She had tied a perfect square knot. "Oh, no!" she sighed. "That'll never do. I don't understand what I did wrong. It looks so easy when your dad does it."

Glancing in the mirror, Cecil muttered, "I can't go looking like this. Let me try it!" While June sat watching him untie the knot, Polly quietly slipped out of the room. Returning in a few minutes, she had their next-door neighbor in tow. "Help is at hand! He's going to do it for you," she announced.

"I remember the first time I had to do this. I didn't know anymore about it then you did," he told Cecil as he fashioned a perfect knot. "With a little practice, it'll be a snap for you, too."

To her surprise, this little episode only strengthened their belief that she could accomplish anything she set out to do. Even though she couldn't figure out how to do it, she'd found a way to get it done before Cecil's friends arrived. That was all he'd asked for. To be on the safe side, though, in case there was no neighbor available the next time Cecil needed to wear a tie, she saw to it Burrel taught him the fine art of tying a Windsor knot.

~

When Polly had so blithely taken on the responsibility of being a mother to June and Cecil, she'd known there would be problems, but nothing had prepared her for the next one. Burrel hadn't warned her of the possibility of them losing their allowances to the slot machines. This was mainly because he was as ignorant of this prospect as she.

That year of 1942, he knew that slot machines were legal in Zanesville, and present in the service station around the corner from where they lived. Never, in his wildest dreams, though, would he have connected these two facts to his offspring.

When June and Cecil first discovered the enticing machine, like magic, it would spit out five, ten or sometimes twenty pennies in exchange for one. This happened often enough to hold out a promise to them of untold riches. When they became sure they couldn't lose, it turned on them until they no longer had any pennies left to feed it.

They lived and breathed for allowance day, so they could start over again. Certain their luck would change, they hurried to the station and dropped penny after penny into the slot and breathlessly waited for the tumblers to revolve. "Please let it be three cherries," was their fervent prayer.

They were unaware that, as minors, their gambling activities were illegal. The young station attendants had known, but ignored what was going on. This state of affairs changed abruptly one evening when the station manager came in early and observed them.

Red faced and angry, he yelled, "What in the name of heaven is going on here?" He was addressing the young attendants as well as June and Cecil. "Don't you know that it's against the law for kids to gamble? I could be fined a lot of money." Then pointing his finger at the attendants, he continued, "You could lose your jobs!"

The station manager was the only one in the room who realized the seriousness of what they had been doing. His tone of voice and his stern expression when he firmly said, "Go home!" left no doubt how unacceptable he considered their behavior.

His final words as they hurried out the door, "I'll be in touch with your parents," made them realize they needed to get home and tell their mom before he did.

Polly was putting the finishing touches on dinner when they burst into the room. "What's the hurry?" she asked, then noticing their flushed faces, she anxiously inquired, "Are you sick?"

Not wasting any time, they told her about their experience with the slot machines and what the station manager had said. She listened quietly, occasionally asking a question or nodding her head. When they'd finished she said, "I'm glad you told me about it before he gets here. At least, this way I'll be prepared."

They were relieved at her reaction, but still worried about having to tell their dad. "Will you talk to Dad?" June asked. Aware of how disappointed he'd be in them, she dreaded getting one of her dad's talking to's.

As it turned out, Polly had already talked to them about the evils of gambling before he got home. What she'd said to them had made such an impression that he didn't find it necessary to say anything at all.

She'd started by asking, "How much of this week's allowance do you have left?" When they replied, "Nothing," she asked, "How much do you have of last week's? What did you buy with it?" Again the answer was, "Nothing."

She continued in this vein until she discovered that all their money was gone, and they hadn't bought anything since the day they'd discovered the slot machines.

"How much money would you have if you hadn't put it in the slot machines?" she asked. "Five dollars," Cecil responded. "How many banana splits could you have gotten with that five dollars?" she asked.

"Lots," June said. "That's not what I asked," Polly responded. "I want you to figure out how many you could have bought with that five dollars."

"Let me see." June said as she used a pencil and piece of paper to work out the problem. "A banana split is thirty-five cents. Divide thirty-five into five-hundred. That's fourteen with ten cents left over."

"I want you two kids to think about what you gave up to play those slot machines. You could each have gone to see fifty movies. June, you could have bought those two sweaters you've had your eye on. Cecil, I'm sure you could have found something more important to do than throw your money away," she continued. "Now let me ask you, what did you get out of playing the slot machines?" she asked.

"We won a little, but we put it back and lost it," Cecil moaned. "We kept thinking, if we played long enough we'd start winning again, but we'd win just enough to keep us going. Then we'd start losing again."

"It's a vicious cycle," Polly said. "I want you to think about this. Maybe it's a good lesson to learn when you're so young. If you gamble your allowance, you're taking a chance you'll have some money, but if you hold onto your allowance it's a sure thing. You'll have the money to save or to buy what you want."

Her words made an impression on them, one they never forgot. Years later, Cecil, as a young sailor, was stationed in a county in Maryland where there were slot machines in every building, except the church. While his buddies were gambling their paychecks, he wasn't even tempted.

Burrel was living close to his brother, Mace, for the first time since nineteen twenty-nine, when he, Priscilla, and baby Cecil had left for their new life in West Virginia. Since only twenty-five miles separated Zanesville and Newark it was now possible for the two families to get together.

During one of Mace's visits, he brought up the subject of Priscilla and Dickie. "You know, it's only seventy-five or eighty miles from here to Mansfield. Aren't you going to try to see Dickie? How about taking June and Cecil to see their mother?"

"She won't let me see him. I guess she's afraid I'll try to take him away from her," Burrel replied. "I was awarded custody, you know."

"I know, but that was in West Virginia. I don't think that court order would apply in Ohio," Mace said.

"Whether it would or not, Priscilla isn't going to take a chance," Burrel responded. "If I can't see Dickie, how can I let her see June and Cecil?"

"How are the kids doing?" Mace asked. "Do they get along with Polly?"

"They get along fine. Sometimes, almost too well. Between the three of them, they really keep me hopping!" Burrel smilingly replied.

"I still can't believe Priscilla left you and the children the way she did," Mace commented.

"You'd better not let Polly hear you say that. She won't let anyone criticize the children's mother. Me included," Burrel said. "We've had some pretty heated discussions about it."

Shaking his head in bewilderment, Mace muttered, "I can't understand why she'd take her side."

"I wouldn't say she's taking her side. She just says the kids have been hurt enough by what people have said. She's not going to let it happen around her," Burrel responded. "I wouldn't recommend tangling with her. She doesn't have that red hair for nothing," he added.

Mace chuckled, "I thought as much. She has a temper, does she?"

Burrel laughingly asked, "Is the sky blue?" Then on a more serious note, "You wouldn't want to get her dander up."

Burrel didn't share with his brother the conversation he'd had with Polly a few nights earlier. He'd been bemoaning the fact that he couldn't see Dickie. "I should go into court and have that custody order enforced," he'd said.

The words were barely out of his mouth when she'd exploded, "How can you even say such a thing? Dickie is the only chick Priscilla has left. You know she can't have any more children. Since you have June and Cecil, how can you even think about taking away the only one she has?"

Her outburst had shocked him into a momentary silence. He hated any kind of unpleasantness, trying always to keep peace in the family.

When she had seen the hurt look in his eyes, she had been sorry for her reaction. "Honey," she'd said, this time in a calmer, more soothing voice, "I didn't mean to upset you, but we have to be realistic about it. You might have legal custody of Dickie, but Priscilla has physical custody. I don't think she's ever going to let you see him until she knows you won't try to take him away."

"You two are adults and need to work out your problems for all three of the children's sake," she'd added. "I'm not sure how Cecil feels. I think that he is still angry at his mother. June, on the other hand, is still hurt. I don't think she'll get over what happened until she can see her mother again."

Quietly mulling over her words, he'd murmured, "I thought she was getting over it. She seems so happy with you. I had the feeling she looked on you as her mother." Then more anxiously, he'd asked, "Don't you think so?"

"No doubt about it. Both kids seem to accept me as a mother, but they still think about Priscilla. I just don't want to see the problems you two have with each other hurt the children."

"I don't either," he'd said. "But so much has happened, I'm going to need more time to work things out."

~

That night, after Polly and the children were asleep, Burrel lie awake thinking of the time a year earlier when his life had fallen apart. Even now, he couldn't believe that Priscilla, his wife, the mother of his children, had left him.

Sleep eluded him as pictures ran through his mind of the night he had returned for the weekend to their home in West Virginia from his job at the shipyard in Baltimore and found the house abandoned. A note on the mantle from his wife Priscilla read, "I have left and taken Dickie with me. June is with your sister, and Cecil is with your father. I'm not coming back, so don't try to find me."

As he tried to keep these memories at bay, he became aware that the only sound in the room was the ticking of the alarm clock, set to go off in 5 hours, and Polly's soft breathing. Afraid his restlessness was going to wake her, he slipped out of bed and padded down the stairs to the kitchen. As he sat at the kitchen table and sipped the warmed-up coffee, he thought about the earlier, happier days he, Priscilla and the children had shared. Images of their life as newlyweds in Ohio flickered through his mind. Mingled with those memories were ones of his years exploring, opening and managing Seneca Caverns and Smokehole Caverns in West Virginia with Priscilla and the children living with him in the house on the hill above the cavern. Then he'd thought he was the luckiest man in the world.

His brother's comments earlier in the day had caused him to relive those days, but he mentally shook himself as his thoughts returned to the present and to Polly still asleep upstairs. Because of her, his life was good again. He had a woman who loved him, and he had his children with him. He sighed as he quietly slipped upstairs and climbed into bed next to her. Before he fell asleep, he decided it was time to let the past go and relax and enjoy his new life.

Their time in Zanesville ran out, though, before the issue of June and Cecil seeing Priscilla could be resolved. Soon they were to be separated by hundreds of miles. The opportunity to bring the children and parents together would soon be as distant as the miles that would keep them apart.

A few nights later, Polly, June, and Cecil waited in anticipation for the sound of familiar steps on the wide front porch. When they finally arrived and the front door opened, they were ready to yell, "Surprise!" Before the words could escape their lips, Burrel beat them to it when he entered the room and called out, "I have a surprise for you!"

Delighted, Polly said, "We didn't think you would remember." Then wrapping her arms around his neck, she murmured, "Happy anniversary, Honey."

Burrel let her words roll around in his mind as he frantically tried to remember what anniversary he had apparently forgotten. Polly and the children in their Sunday best, the party decorations, and the glowing candles on the table made him aware he had forgotten an occasion important to his family. For the life of him, though, he couldn't remember what it could be.

Especially attuned to her father's feelings since they had been reunited, June was the first to realize Burrel's predicament. She quickly filled in the gaps for him when she announced, "It is hard to believe that we have been a family for three months today, isn't it, Dad?"

He rewarded his daughter with a quick smile before he echoed Polly's words, "Happy Anniversary." As they sat around the dining room table and he listened to the happy chatter around him, not for the first time, he counted his blessings. It was difficult to believe that only three months earlier, this family had been separated by miles. Now thanks to this red-headed young woman sitting across from him, they were a family again.

During a loll in the conversation, Polly remembered Burrel's pronouncement that he had something for them. Not seeing a gaily wrapped gift, curiosity got the better of her, and she asked what his surprise was. Stunned silence greeted him when he announced, "Since my job here in Zanesville has just ended, I've taken a new job outside of Washington, D.C., and I have to be there in a week."

While the rest of the family absorbed his words, tears spilled down June's cheeks. This was too reminiscent of what had happened before when their original family circle had been forever shattered. She didn't think she could bear the thought of again being separated from her father. Was it possible that this family, like her other one, was being broken before it had a chance to begin?

Becoming aware of his daughter's unhappiness, Burrel tousled her blonde hair and reassured her that this time, they were all going together. "With the war just started, there will be a lot of defense construction going on. At first, I will be working on a new army base. This time, there won't be any house hunting. We are going as a family." After a short pause, he added, "And we are taking our house with us!"

Thus began their vagabond years.

CHAPTER TWO

PERILOUS JOURNEY

The United States involvement in the war was increasing. Every day brought news of the fighting in Europe and on some previously unheard of islands in the South Pacific. During President Roosevelt's "Fireside Chats" with the American people, he encouraged everyone to work together to bring this terrible war to an end.

Factories were geared up to make planes, tanks, and other military supplies. Millions of men were being drafted, among them Burrel's nephews, Garth and Merlin, from West Virginia. More military bases were being built as temporary quarters for the men who were being trained to fight this world engulfing war.

For the first time in over a decade, there were more available jobs than men to fill them. This marked the beginning of an era, one where women moved out of the kitchen into the war plants. A new term "Rosie The Riveter" was introduced to describe this new breed of women.

June and Cecil's mother, Priscilla, had become one of these women. Over a year ago, after she had left West Virginia, she had boarded a bus with eight year old Dickie and gone to Mansfield, Ohio. At first she worked at Max's Diner, but later began working as a salad girl in the cafeteria at the Westinghouse factory.

As more workers were needed for the war effort, Priscilla again changed jobs, going from making salads to testing ammunition shells at a factory called the Dominion. Sitting at a workbench, she spent her days dipping the shells into a container of water to be sure they were leak proof. Although the work was tedious, it was her way of contributing to the war effort.

Her future husband, Bill, who had followed them from West Virginia had gotten a job at the Westinghouse plant in Mansfield. Previously manufacturing refrigerators, stoves, and other major household appliances, the factory now turned out bombsights along with other defense related products.

∼

Many defense construction projects were either on the drawing boards or in actual construction. As a full-fledged new member of the union, Burrel had access to the availability of these positions. He had been excited when his bid had been accepted for the job as an electrician at the defense construction site outside Washington, D.C. in Beltsville, Maryland.

At the union hall he had heard horror stories about the lack of housing near these construction sites. Being separated again from his family was not a prospect he had relished. He knew that he had to come up with a way to keep his family together. Pondering his options, he found himself thinking about the travel trailer Priscilla's sister and her husband had brought to the cavern a few years ago. It had been cozy and compact, but best of all, it had allowed them to be mobile.

Talking to other men at the union hall, he had learned this was a solution others had come up with to avoid leaving their families behind.

∼

The family had been leery when he had announced his surprise that they were packing up and moving their house and becoming vagabonds. They had been receptive, though, when he had explained that the house they would be moving would be a trailer. They were all glad they were going to be on this adventure together.

Within a couple days they found and purchased a trailer. Twenty feet long and eight feet wide, the exterior was blue with an interior paneled in a blonde colored wood. There was not one inch of wasted space. Like bookends, each end of the trailer had a living area with a couch surrounded by built-in shelves and overhead cabinets. These sections became the bedrooms at night. The transformation was accomplished with a few deft movements, resulting in the couch being changed into a bed.

In the center was a kitchen with a small stove, sink, refrigerator, storage cupboards, and a table and chairs. A sliding door divided the trailer into two rooms, and provided a little bit of privacy.

Though Polly was happy to leave the big house, June and Cecil walked through the spacious rooms saying a reluctant goodbye. Leaving for the last time, June looked back and thought of the good times they'd had here. Packed with their other belongings were the few snapshots they had taken of their life in this house. Just as vivid, though, were the memories of these last few months indelibly etched in her mind.

During their last few days in Zanesville they found themselves enmeshed in a flurry of activities. Arrangements had to be made for the transfer of June and Cecil's school records and goodbyes had to be said.

Addresses and promises to keep in touch were exchanged with friends they had made, but before the words were out of her mouth, June realized these were promises she wouldn't keep. Like the friends she'd left behind in West Virginia, she knew they were out of her life, forever.

This wasn't the case, when they visited Mace, Mabel, Inez, Rose, and Annamae in Newark. This family would always be a part of their lives. Although they would make and leave many friends in the next few years, they had the security of knowing that these friends, their cousins, would always be there for them. They were exceptionally close since Inez was the same age as Cecil, Rose as June, and Annamae as Dickie.

They were all filled with excitement and anticipation as moving day approached. Everything was in readiness. Since all the closet and cabinet doors were fastened with security latches, everything could remain in its designated space. No packing was necessary.

"Tomorrow is the big day!" Burrel said. "All we have to do now is hook the trailer to the car and we'll be on our way."

"I just hope we don't get any more snow," Polly commented. "That's one thing I won't miss about Ohio. This blasted snow!"

We Were Vagabonds

"Spoken like a true southerner!" Burrel replied. "This winter hasn't been half bad. I've seen a lot worse," he added.

"It's bad enough for me," she replied. "I can't imagine how it could be any worse than this."

The snow was falling when they got out of bed the next morning. Peering out the front window, Burrel said, "This doesn't look good to me. I wonder what the weather forecast is."

Turning the radio dial, he found a weather report. Periods of heavy snow were predicted, dwindling to snow flurries by noon. "That doesn't sound too bad," Burrel said. "The weatherman said the trucks are already out, plowing and salting the roads. If we give it a little time, they should have them cleared in a couple hours."

He might have postponed their departure another day, if he hadn't been scheduled to report for work Monday morning. Since this was Friday, he would need to leave today to give them time to get there and find a place to get the trailer situated, before he had to go to work.

～

As the weatherman had predicted, the heavy snow had changed to flurries by the time they were on the road. The route they would be traveling was Route 40, also known as the National Road. This would connect them with the Pennsylvania Turnpike, a new four-lane toll highway.

"We'll make much better time once we get to the turnpike," Burrel told them as he negotiated the curves on the steep hill leading out of Zanesville. "The roads are worse than I thought they would be," he muttered.

"Do you think we should go back?" Polly inquired, anxiously, before adding, "That's the last time I'm going to say I can't imagine anything worse. These roads are worse than anything I've ever seen."

They rode along in silence for a while, Burrel concentrating on his driving, and the rest of the family watching the road for him. As they continued, they saw skid marks and an occasional vehicle that had skidded off the road.

Burrel was a good driver and had years of experience driving on roads worse than this, so everyone in the car had confidence in him and in his ability to get them safely to their destination.

Everything was going fine until twenty-five miles from Zanesville they came to the small town of Cambridge. Entering the town, he felt an almost imperceptible swing of the trailer when he drove down an extremely steep hill.

"That hill reminded me of home," he chuckled. "I can tell you, I'm glad to have that one behind me."

They were all talking and laughing as they approached a bridge. Like no bridge they'd ever seen, it appeared to go straight up into the air. "That's a steep one," Burrel said, as he shifted into low, and started up this man-made incline.

"We're stuck!" he said, as he tried to accelerate. Disgusted, he added, "I can't go anywhere. I don't know what good it's going to do for the drivers in back of me to keep blowing their horns."

Glancing in the rear view mirror at the line of cars behind them, he said, "I'm not going to be able to move this car and trailer without some help." No sooner were the words out of his mouth than Polly opened the car door and jumped out. While they watched she ran from car to car, saying, "We have two kids in the car and we're stuck. Can you help us?"

Men, some in suits and topcoats, others in work clothes piled out of their vehicles. Making their way over the snow-covered pavement, they hurried to the car. Standing, three on each side, they tried to push it. They might have succeeded, if it hadn't been for the attached trailer.

By then June and Cecil had gotten out and were standing watching the men's unsuccessful efforts. Drawn by the noise and flurry of activity, other travelers and town people gathered to watch them. One woman drew laughter when she muttered, "We haven't had this much excitement around here since the circus was in town."

Burrel was beginning to despair of ever getting out of this situation, when a city truck, its yellow lights flashing, pulled up beside him. "Mister, sit tight. We're going to get you off this bridge," the driver announced.

Matching action to his words, he and his co-workers grabbed shovels from the back of the truck and started to heap ashes under the wheels. "This won't take long," a man, obviously in charge, announced. "Just tell me, Mister, what kind of a fool idea was it to bring that contraption out on a day like this?"

Burrel wasn't angry. He'd been sitting here for an hour thinking much the same thing. One thing for sure, this was the last time he was going to believe the weatherman.

Shortly after their rescuers arrived, Burrel was able to get enough traction to finish the trip across the bridge. He had received his orders from the city workers and the police to, "Pull that blasted thing over as soon as you get off the bridge. You can park it there during the night. By morning we'll have the streets clear and you can leave town."

"I guess they mean it," Burrel said as he pulled over to the curb. Any doubt he might have had was allayed by the presence of the patrol car stopping behind him.

Stepping out of the car, the burly officer said, "This is the last time we want to have to rescue you. You've caused enough excitement for one day."

Burrel assured the officer they wouldn't have any more trouble with the Harmans. "I appreciate all the help you gave us, but we're glad to call it a day." The little family breathed a sigh of relief, as standing by their trailer home, they watched the patrol car drive away.

Unhitching the trailer, they stood back and surveyed their surroundings. They were parked in the shadow of the bridge next to a billboard of Uncle Sam. Splashed across the sign, large letters proclaimed, "UNCLE SAM NEEDS YOU!"

~

That evening after the snow quit falling, June, Cecil, and Polly built a snowman under the billboard of Uncle Sam. Before going into the warmth of their snug home, Cecil threw a snowball at June and she retaliated. Polly came to June's defense and Cecil was momentarily outnumbered. About ready to run for cover, he was surprised to hear his dad say, "Think they have you, do they? Let's see how they do now." Laughing he picked up some snow, formed it into a ball, and let it fly.

Polly had been stooped over scooping up more snow, making her derriere a perfect target. "Gotcha," Burrel yelled, as his well-aimed missile made a perfect hit.

Straightening up, she blistered the air with a few well-chosen words before plastering him with a hail of snowballs. By then, Cecil and June had joined in the fray.

Laughingly, the battle continued until they became aware their activities were attracting almost as much attention as they had on the bridge. Drivers were slowing down and honking their horns, and a few passersby had stopped to watch.

"Let's call a truce," Polly said. "I'm afraid we've drawn quite an audience." As Burrel, June, and Cecil abandoned their cache of snowballs, she added, "Besides, the macaroni and cheese should be about done by now."

She had put the casserole in the oven before going outside. They had returned in time to find it done to perfection. "If we'd stayed out a few minutes longer, I'd have been serving you burnt offerings," she quipped.

As they sat around the table, the food and hot chocolate warming their stomachs, they talked about the day's events. "What a day!" Burrel exclaimed. "It seemed like a disaster, but turned into quite an adventure." They all heartily agreed as they cleared off the table and got ready for bed.

The trailer, snug and cozy, felt like home. Being parked on a street in a strange town, with the picture of Uncle Sam looking down on them didn't change that. In that period of time between wakefulness and sleep, realization came to June that the people in it made a house a home. This trailer wasn't as spacious as some houses she'd lived in, but it held a very important ingredient, one she'd found hard to live without. It was full of love and people caring for each other.

~

It didn't take long the next morning, to discern that the temperature had taken a drop during the night. As Burrel and Cecil refastened the trailer hitch, the wind was whipping through their warm, heavy clothing. Coming back into the trailer, Burrel announced, "The snow has stopped and the roads are clear. We shouldn't have any trouble, but you girls had better put some heavy clothes on. It's going to be really cold today."

The wind swirled around them as soon as they stepped out of the trailer. "You weren't kidding," Polly said, as she quickly dashed for the protection of the car. "At least we won't have to worry about it as long as we're inside."

They hadn't gone far when they realized the fallacy of her statement. The cold seemed to seep through the floorboards and windows of the old car. Although the heater was operating full blast, it was no match for the sub-zero temperatures.

Pulling the trailer slowed their progress. "We can't stand much more of this cold," Burrel said. "We're almost to little Washington," he added, referring to Washington, Pennsylvania. "We'll stop there and get some blankets out of the trailer. I'm afraid to pull over here. We might get stuck in the snow."

Arriving in little Washington, they stopped at a restaurant for some hot food and a chance to get warm. "My feet are so cold, they're almost numb," Polly said. "Mine, too," June and Cecil echoed.

They emptied the trailer of all their blankets and pulled on extra socks, before continuing their journey. After they had bundled themselves in the warmth of the blankets, Polly commented, "That should help us, but what about you, Burrel?"

"I'll be alright," he said. "I have to have my arms free so I can drive. If this wind would just ease up, we'd be okay." He could feel the car and trailer swaying from side to side, and there were times he feared he wouldn't be able to keep it on the road.

By the time they'd entered the Pennsylvania turnpike they were again feeling the effects of the cold. "We're going to have to stop, so we can get warm," Polly said. "Do you think there will be any restaurants or filling stations on this road?"

"There's something!" Cecil yelled, as he sighted the bright orange roof of a building in the distance. "It looks like a restaurant." As they drew nearer they could see a low white building topped in bright orange. This was the first time any of them had seen a Howard Johnson restaurant, and it was a most welcome sight.

The building was full of travelers, some looking as cold as the four of them felt. They trooped in, thankful to escape from the chill. Sitting in the booth, engulfed in the warmth of the restaurant, they consumed hot soup and cheeseburgers. They didn't leave the comfort of the restaurant until the pain had ebbed from their toes.

These restaurants became a safe haven for them for the rest of their trip. They stopped at every one. Between meals the adults would drink coffee, and the children would have hot chocolate. None of them availed themselves of the specialty of the house, the twenty-six flavors of ice cream. At any other time this would have been a treat, but not on this trip.

~

It was two o'clock in the morning when they got to the outskirts of Washington, D.C. As they drove into town, everything was closed except The Hot Shoppe, one of a chain of restaurants in the Washington area. They were surprised at the scene that greeted them at this time of night. All the booths were full, and there were only a few empty stools at the counter. Music was blaring from the jukebox, and customers and waitresses were bustling about, talking and laughing.

A man at the counter scooted over so they could all sit together. "What'll you have?" the counterman asked Burrel.

"Two coffees and two hot chocolates," Polly said to the waiting counterman. Then patting Burrel on the arm, she added, "We're all so tired, we can hardly think straight. I think we'd better find a place to park so we can get a good night's sleep."

They quickly downed their drinks and started off on the search for a place to stay. Not finding anything more suitable, Burrel pulled into the lot of a darkened gas station. "This is going to have to do," he said. "We'll find something permanent tomorrow."

As the heat from the oil stove quickly heated the interior, they were thankful the trailer was so small as it only took a few minutes for it to become warm and comfortable.

Although the cold they had experienced on the trip had left Polly and June with near frostbitten toes, neither had any permanent damage, but they did suffer its effects for a long time to come.

Arriving to open the station the next morning, the manager was surprised to see the trailer, but he wasn't upset. After Burrel told him about their experiences of the previous day, the man was very helpful, directing them to a nearby trailer court on the outskirts of town, not too far from Burrel's job.

After they rented a space and set up the trailer, they drove around checking out the town, locating the school June and Cecil would be attending and the construction site where Burrel would be working.

Early the next morning, he left for his new job and June and Cecil for school. At the bus stop they met some students whose fathers also worked at the construction site. Like June and Cecil these children were becoming accustomed to going from one school to another because of their fathers' jobs.

Two of the girls were in June's grade, and one of the boys was in Cecil's. Knowing what it felt like to be the new kid in the school, these new friends went out of their way to make the newcomers feel welcome.

The girls were opposites in appearance. Nadia was short with a square compact build, blue eyes and short saucy curls. Brown eyed, Joy was slender and of average height. She wore her dark hair in a smooth pageboy.

While they waited for the bus, June discovered that, like her dad, her new friends' fathers had all left jobs back home to go on the road with their families. They were all following the big construction jobs as their part in the war effort. When Nadia introduced herself, she said, "We moved here from Pennsylvania where my father was a tenant farmer. He's only been doing construction work for a few months but this is my second school this year."

"Mine too," Joy said before she added, "My father worked in a hardware store in Upper New York before we went on the road."

To the other girls' surprise, June announced, "My father was a caveman."

"He was not! I saw your father last night and he's not old enough to be a caveman!" Nadia exclaimed.

June laughed and told them about her father's history as a cave explorer and how he had explored and opened Smokehole and Seneca Caverns in West Virginia.

When they got to their classrooms, she didn't feel as uncomfortable being introduced to the class as she had in Zanesville. Having familiar faces smiling their encouragement made it easier. Later, her newfound friends walked to class with her and invited her to join them for lunch in the cafeteria. Both girls were friendly, warm, and full of fun, and June was looking forward to getting to know them better.

~

She soon found out, though, this was not to be. "We're moving," Polly told them when they got home.

Her words stopped June and Cecil in their tracks, their faces mirrored the amazement they felt. "Moving? What do you mean? We just got here!" June cried.

"Things didn't work out on your dad's job," she responded. "He quit. Before he came home he stopped at the union hall and got another job. He's going to be working on the construction of a big government building called the Pentagon in Washington, D.C. We're going to have to move closer to his work."

June was filled with contradictory feelings, disappointment at the thought of leaving Nadia and Joy and excitement at the prospect of living even closer to Washington, D.C.

Burrel had no inkling when he'd arrived at his new job that morning that he'd be quitting before the day was over. The work was familiar and not particularly difficult, and the other men appeared to be congenial. Later in the day, though, while walking up the steps behind his foreman, he'd overheard him complaining to another man, "I don't have anything but son-of-a-bitches working on this job."

Although usually slow to anger, this statement made Burrel furious since, to him, calling a man a son-of-a-bitch was an insult to his mother. The foreman could have said anything except that, and he would have shrugged it off.

Tapping the foreman on the shoulder, he grimly muttered, "This is one son-of-a-bitch you won't have to worry about. I quit." Having said this, he'd gone to the personnel office, officially resigned, and picked up his pay.

CHAPTER THREE

A NEW LIFESTYLE

Now that he'd found the job at the Pentagon, he faced a dilemma. He still felt strongly that he didn't want to raise the children in a big city, so he would have to find a place to live in one of the outlying areas. Checking with other electricians at the Washington local union, he found out about a trailer court in Bladensburg, Maryland that sounded like what he wanted. Although it was only a few miles outside the city, the area had all the characteristics of a small town. Living there would mean he'd have a long drive to work through the Washington traffic. While he wasn't looking forward to it, he knew it would be the right thing to do for his family.

Living in a trailer park was a new experience, one to which they soon adjusted. The owner of the court, a single mother with two children to support had turned the acreage behind her house into a small trailer court. Fifteen plots, each twenty-five by fifty feet had been laid out. Each one had its own water and electric hook up and accommodated one trailer. Located near the entrance to the court was a large cement block building that housed the community laundry and shower facilities.

The court itself was like a small community with everyone knowing each other. Most of the men worked on construction sites around Washington, and like Burrel they found living in a trailer the only way to keep their families together.

As the women met in the washhouse and swapped stories about their vagabond lives, none could top Polly's tale of moving after just one day.

Three months into the year June and Cecil were in their third school. They found Maryland's school system unlike any they had ever attended. One less year was required to complete a high school education. Students graduated from grade school at the end of the seventh grade. Eighth graders were considered high school freshmen. Then at the end of the eleventh grade, students would graduate from high school. June was amazed to realize she would be a high school freshman next year while she was still twelve years old. If they stayed in Maryland, she would be a fifteen-year-old senior.

Both Cecil and June made friends in the trailer court rather than in school. June's best friend was the daughter of the owner of the park, and Cecil's was the son of a construction worker. On Saturdays the four of them would walk a mile to Kennilsworth, Maryland, board a trolley, and ride into Washington, D.C. Most Saturdays would find them browsing through the Smithsonian Institute or National Museum of Natural Science. They would stare in awe at Lindbergh's airplane, The Spirit of St. Louis, hanging from the ceiling. The displays of prehistoric people triggered their imaginations. Walking alongside skeletons of dinosaurs made them feel dwarfed.

Other times they'd go to a movie at one of the downtown theaters. For the twenty-five cent admission they could sit in the darkened theater and watch their favorite stars flick across the screen. They'd never miss a movie starring Betty Grable, Lana Turner, Clark Gable, Tyrone Powers, Barbara Stanwick, or Robert Taylor.

Following the movie would be a live stage show. One week they got to see and hear Jimmy Dorsey and his big band. Another time Basil Rathbone, the star of the Sherlock Holmes movies, read poetry. Always there were acrobats, comics, singers, tap dancers, and a sing-a-long.

～

Having missed Gone With The Wind when it was first released, they decided to attend it one Sunday as a family. They arrived early in the capital city, in order to find a parking space, but soon discovered they hadn't been the only ones with that idea. There were no empty parking spaces close to the theater.

Burrel drove for several blocks before he was able to find one. Not wanting to be late, they hurried out of the car and walked quickly to the theater. Arriving as the opening credits flashed onto the screen, they settled into their seats and immediately became absorbed in the movie.

Sometime within the four hours before the final scene Polly's feet started hurting, and she kicked off her shoes. When the movie was over and they got up to leave, she couldn't find them. After much searching, Cecil triumphantly held them up, "Got them!" he proclaimed.

By now the theater had emptied and was beginning to refill as people were arriving for the second show. "Come on. Get them on," Burrel urged. "I don't want to get caught in this stampede."

Taking the shoes from Cecil's outstretched hand, she replied, "I'll only be a minute." Then there was silence.

"I thought you said, you'd only be a minute," Burrel grumbled. "What's taking so long?"

"I can't get them on," she replied with a sigh, "My feet are swollen, and my shoes don't fit."

Sitting beside her, taking a shoe in his hand, he said, "Are you sure?" As he tried to force her foot into it, the shoe appeared to be at least two sizes too small. Although he struggled along with her, there was no way those swollen feet were going to fit into those shoes.

"What are we going to do, Mom?" Cecil asked. Not anxious to sit through the movie again, he protested. "We can't just stay here all night!"

"We sure can't," she responded. "I'm just going to walk out of here in my stocking feet. Here, Burrel," she said. "You can carry my shoes."

The adventure wasn't over. When they exited the theater, no one could remember where they'd parked the car. Polly, walking barefooted, Burrel with a high-heeled pump dangling from each hand, and June and Cecil walking alongside drew many a sidelong glance from people passing by.

After searching first in one direction, then another they finally spotted it. No one was any happier to see it than Polly. By now, the soles of her stockings were full of runs, and her feet were beginning to bleed. She sighed with relief as she sank into the comfort of the car.

Everyone could have been grouchy after the incidents of the day, but they remained in good spirits. Other than feeling sorry for Polly with her sore feet, they all saw the humor in their experiences. This was another day that wove them tighter together as a family.

~

Their first Easter together was a bright sunny day, a vivid contrast to the gloom on June and Cecil's faces. Trying to act nonchalant, they'd quickly scanned the trailer looking for their Easter baskets. Given the size of their home, it didn't take long for them to discover there were none to be found.

Observing their disappointed faces, Polly had a sinking feeling she and Burrel had made a mistake in thinking they were too old for Easter baskets. "I'm afraid we goofed," she told Burrel. "Do you think we could find any place open today where we could find some baskets?"

"It won't be easy. It's hard enough finding anything open on a regular Sunday. I imagine it will be almost impossible on Easter Sunday," he replied. "Let's have some breakfast. Then we can all go see what we can find."

They started their treasure hunt in high spirits, first driving through the streets of Bladensburg. Finding nothing open except churches, they decided to go into Washington. Finally, about ready to admit defeat, they spotted a small drug store with a sign in the window proclaiming "We're Open."

Not taking any chances of it closing before they had a chance to get inside, after Burrel pulled over to the curb, they scrambled out and hurried into the store. Then to Polly's query, "Do you have any Easter baskets?" the clerk responded, "I think we're all sold out."

"Let's see if there's any Easter candy left," Polly said as she started walking through the aisles. "It looks to me as if we're going to have to make do. That would be better than nothing."

Standing, scanning the candy filled shelves, she exclaimed, "I've found something!" This announcement quickly brought the other three to her side. All eyes turned to the small, perfectly shaped basket she was holding. Full of candy bunnies, eggs, and jellybeans, the entire basket was made of chocolate. They had never seen anything quite like it.

Exiting the store, holding these delicious confections were two happy children. This day was truly one to be stored away in their memories.

Years later, Sammy Davis, a popular singer, had a hit song called "The Candy Man". Every time June heard him sing the line about being able to eat the dishes, she would remember that Easter of nineteen forty-two. Not only the remembrance of the chocolate Easter basket, but the love and caring shown by their parents that day so long ago, still remains, clear and bright as another echo in her mind.

～

Since he hadn't had the opportunity for as much formal schooling as he would have liked, their father put great store in education. This lack had caused him to spend his life trying to make up for it. "There are things out there to see and people to meet. If you kids will just keep your eyes and ears open, you'll learn a lot," he told them. "We are going to have to move again when school is out. The job at the Pentagon is almost finished. Wherever we go we'll be meeting new people and you'll make new friends. It will be an education for all of us."

While still living close to Washington, they took advantage of the opportunities in the area for learning. They went into town often, taking in the sights and visiting the monuments. They never failed to be awed by the majesty of the statue of a seated Abraham Lincoln inside the columned Lincoln Memorial. The view from the steps of this structure showed the mirrored image of the Washington Monument in the clear waters of the reflection pool. Its beauty always impressed them.

This was especially true when the cherry blossoms were in bloom. Remembering that these trees had been a gift of the Japanese people during a more peaceful time didn't dim their beauty or people's enjoyment of them. It certainly didn't effect the Harman family's pleasure the day they came into the city to see them. The trees provided a triple treat, first the sight of the blossoms, then their reflection in the pool. All this splendor was accompanied by a sweet, pleasant aroma, one so strong it permeated their skin and soaked into their clothing.

Before going home, they, like thousands of tourists before them, took pictures of each other with the cherry blossoms as a background.

In that spring of nineteen forty-two in Washington, D.C. there was also history in the making. New government offices were being created to handle a country at war. Young women from all over the country were pouring into the capital to handle the increased amount of work these new departments generated. Another new word was coined to describe these working women. They were called "government girls".

Noontime and after office hours the streets would be full of government girls. Watching them pass by, they appeared glamorous in their pretty dresses and well coifed hair. She envied her older cousins Irene, Avanelle and Maxine who had joined their ranks. It was not surprising that immersed in the ambiance of the times, her one goal was to grow up and be a government girl. When she voiced this thought to Polly, she was told she'd grow up fast enough, not to wish her life away.

All around the city there was a heightened sense of excitement and purpose. The streets were full of service men on weekend passes. Some were stationed at one of the new bases nearby while others were passing through on their way overseas.

~

The family's favorite place to visit was Mount Vernon, George Washington's home. Though actual travel time from their house was little more than an hour, once they arrived they felt as if they had taken a century and a half journey into the past.

Furthering this illusion were the plantation's employees. Most of them were grandfatherly men in their sixties. Their pace slow and relaxed, they could be found either ambling along beside the visitors or sitting on the many comfortable benches that were scattered throughout the grounds. Their behavior created the illusion that they were personal friends of the Washington family.

It was difficult to imagine by listening to them talk, that the residents of this beautiful home had been dead since the eighteenth century. When she heard them make comments such as, "This building is full of the general's carriages." Or, "This was the general's favorite room," June had the feeling that, at any moment, George Washington might come striding through the door. She was especially to remember one guard who, while standing with them by the wharf, talked about the general's famous visitors who had docked at this landing. Listening, really feeling a part of history, she knew this was what her dad had been talking about when he'd told them how much they could learn outside the classroom.

Years later, when June returned with her husband and children, she was saddened to see this relaxed atmosphere had vanished. Aloof young men in smart looking uniforms had replaced their friendly hosts. Their behavior made it evident, this was merely a tourist attraction, and that George Washington was a long dead historical figure.

No longer did you feel you could leisurely stroll through the rooms of the house, meander through the grounds, or stand by the wharf or on the veranda watching as the Potomac River flowed by.

Those who tried to take their time were likely to hear a harsh voice command, "Keep it moving. You're holding up the line." June experienced this herself, on this later visit, when she'd been trying to take a picture inside the kitchen, and she'd been told "You can't take pictures in here. Keep the line moving."

How much more educational it had been, that spring of nineteen forty-two, when the employees had made their beloved "General Washington" come alive for them.

~

June's seventh grade graduation day arrived, and as she proudly accepted her diploma, her eyes sought and found her family applauding loudly in the fourth row. She was torn between feeling proud and embarrassed by the attention they were receiving. If an award had been given for the loudest applause, her family would have received it.

This was another milestone in her life. She was going to be a high school freshman at the young age of twelve. Her dad had announced earlier to the family that he had completed his part of the job of installing the electrical work in the new Pentagon building. June knew it was time to move again, so she was seeing her fellow students for the last time. Not having made close friends in the school made it easier to walk away without a thought of looking back.

Leaving the trailer park was a different matter. She and Cecil both had friends here. Even their dad's pep talk about all the people they were about to meet didn't ease the pain of knowing they would never see these friends again.

His announcement that they were going into town to buy a new car helped take their minds off their impending departure. Since the automobile factories were converting to manufacturing tanks and other vehicles for the armed services, this meant no cars would be produced until after the war was over.

"This old car isn't going to hold up much longer," Burrel told them one evening over dinner. "If we're going to buy one, it's going to have to be now."

As he talked, Polly looked pensive. "We don't have the money," she said. "I don't know how we're going to be able to afford it now. If we could wait a few months, it would be better."

"I agree with you on that," he responded, "But if we wait, there probably won't be any new cars to buy." He was right, but it was hard for any of them to fathom that cars would no longer be rolling off the assembly lines.

They had just gone into debt to buy a larger trailer since even Polly, who liked small cozy places, had found their twenty-footer too small. The new purchase had been brought about because she and Burrel needed more privacy. While she was frank in her discussions with June and Cecil about the facts of life, she hadn't wanted them to overhear her more intimate moments with their father.

Most children living in the trailers of the nineteen forties were more aware of their parents' amorous activities than any parent imagined. A standard joke was, "That must have been a bad storm last night, the way the trailer shook." Having the larger trailer assured the children wouldn't overhear anything from the front bedroom, but it didn't do much to avert the frequent storms they experienced.

Choosing the car was a family affair. They spent one Saturday going to the different dealerships until they found the car they liked and could afford. It was a Chevrolet with a streamlined body style called the "Torpedo". It was painted in two tones, the lower part tan and the top brown.

The price tag of eight hundred dollars seemed like a fortune to them. Although the adults still worried about going further into debt, they were proud of their first new car. As they sank into the soft seats and inhaled the new car smell, they felt that whether they were able to afford it or not, this was pure luxury.

They soon discovered the car was more of a necessity than an extravagance. It seemed, for the next few years, that Burrel always had to drive long distances to and from work.

～

One day, before they moved, when Burrel arrived home, he found a worried Polly waiting for him. "What's wrong, Honey?" he asked.

"It's Cecil. He left here this morning on his bicycle and hasn't come back," she responded. "He just said he was going for a ride. I never dreamed he'd be gone all day."

Though he was disturbed, Burrel didn't want to distress her any more than she already was. "You know how boys are. He probably went off somewhere with a friend. You know Cecil. He'll be home when it's time to eat."

He had no sooner finished speaking than the object of their discussion pedaled into the front yard. Letting his bicycle drop to the ground, he sauntered into the trailer saying, "What's for dinner?"

His question was met by a spate of angry words from Polly. "Where have you been? What do you mean being gone so long? I pictured you lying dead by the side of the road."

"Whew!" he thought, "I've really got her redheaded temper going." Looking calmer than he felt, he replied, "I just rode into Washington. I didn't think anyone would be worried."

"Into Washington!" she cried. "You actually rode your bike into downtown Washington! I can't believe it!" A frightened look crossed her face when she added, "Don't you know you could have been hit by a car?"

"Calm down, Polly," Burrel said. "Let me talk to him." This was worse than Cecil thought. He was going to get one of his dad's dreaded "talking to's".

This one started out, "Son, don't you know how dangerous it is to ride a bicycle in all that city traffic? You could have been hurt. Your mother has a right to be upset. I trusted you to use better judgment than that. You have no idea how bad I feel having to talk to you like this." He continued this particular "talking to" in his soft, calm voice, every word making Cecil ashamed of what he had done.

By the time Burrel was through, there was no need to punish Cecil. He was sincerely contrite; never again did he want to put his father through such an ordeal. His dad's talks always had this effect. Then when they went inside for supper, Polly wanted to continue talking about it, but Burrel softly said, "It's been taken care of." That was the end of the discussion.

However, that wasn't the end of the day's excitement. While they were finishing their dessert, and listening to the radio, they heard the wail of a siren. Burrel announced, "It's the air raid alarm. June, turn off the lights." Polly said, "Cecil, help us pull the curtains." As they sat in the darkness, hearing the blare of the siren, the reality of the war struck close to home.

Then when they walked outside and watched the searchlights criscrossing the sky, a neighbor joined them and asked, "Do you think it is really a raid?"

"I don't think so," Burrel replied. "We were just listening to the radio. It seems to me, planes couldn't get this far without being seen. If any of the air raid wardens had spotted them, there would have been a warning over the radio."

Although they all agreed with his reasoning, they were still uneasy. "I heard that if the Germans or Japs attacked us, it would probably be right here in the capital," another neighbor remarked.

By now several others had gathered around. "I heard that trailers look like tanks from the air," someone said. "That doesn't make me feel too safe, does it you?" Several people murmured that they hadn't heard it, but that sounded right to them. The park's children had been anxiously watching the sky and were relieved when the "all clear" was sounded. Air raid alarms weren't new to them. Since war had been declared, several drills had been held in their schools. When the alarm was sounded, they either crawled under their desks or into their lockers where they sat with their heads cradled in their arms until hearing it was safe to come out.

Fortunately for children in this country, all they were to experience were drills. This wasn't the case with children in most other parts of the world. As she had for so many years, June still prayed for God to keep those children safe.

Although she had no way of knowing it at the time, someday some of these people in her prayers would become very important in her life. While she and her classmates were participating in these air raid drills, there was a little German girl exactly her age who was living through the real nightmares of war in Berlin. Though their countries were enemies now, in the future June and this German girl, Heidi Masnick, were to become true friends brought together by the marriage of June's daughter to Heidi's son.

In Manchuria there was a young Japanese girl living with her parents whose mother was dressing her as a boy to protect her from their enemies. Though as children their countries were in bitter conflict now, one day June and this little girl, Yoko Okada, would become very close friends and sisters-in-law.

In war torn Lithuania a young doctor and his wife would be fleeing to America to save their lives. Years later June would have special ties to this young couple, Juozas and Valerija Masilionis, through the marriage of June's son to their daughter and the birth of their grandchildren. All over the world, lives were being torn apart by the war, but in the future all these young people would be brought together by love.

CHAPTER FOUR
THEIR GYPSY SUMMER

When moving day arrived, the family found the all too familiar scene repeating itself as they left for yet another new home. June and Cecil waved to their friends from the back seat as Burrel slowly maneuvered the car and trailer onto the highway. To the unspoken question, "Will we ever see them again?" June's mind responded with a resounding, "No!" These people, they'd shared so many good times with, were now part of the past. As their friends disappeared from view, June seemed to wrap herself in a protective coating, one that over the years would shield her from the pain of these goodbyes.

They all liked the new place Burrel had found. It was a beautiful spot on the tree-shaded grounds of a small country hostel called "Bush River Inn." Not a regular court, the owners had set up facilities for only four trailers. Located alongside the banks of the Susquehanna River, their spot was nestled among the trees. The shade of their wide branches protected them from the merciless summer sun. The park in Bladensburg hadn't afforded this protection.

June was awakened the first morning in their new home, by the nearby clamor of warfare. The sound of "Boom! Boom! Boom!" reverberated in her ears. These noises were familiar. She had heard them many times in war movies or newsreels. Sitting up in bed, she cried out, "What is it? Is it an attack?" As she got up and looked out the window, she was faced with nothing more frightening than the sight of her dad, lunch box in hand, standing by the open door of his car.

Polly, still in her robe, was reaching up to kiss him goodbye. Neither seemed the least bit alarmed. "This isn't real. I must have been dreaming!" she thought. The sound again echoed through the structure. "Boom! Boom! Boom!" This time she could feel a slight vibration under her bare feet. "Mom, Dad, what is it?" she called through the open window.

Seeing her alarmed face peering out at them Burrel replied, "It's alright. That's coming from the Aberdeen Proving Grounds. The army is testing guns. Sometimes the sound will travel, and we'll be able to hear them here. I was talking to our neighbors, and they said they're used to it. They hardly ever hear it anymore."

Reassured by his words, June decided she might as well stay up and start exploring the area. "Get up, you sleepy head," she said to her brother. "How can you sleep through all this noise?"

"Oh, that!" he replied. "They're just testing the big guns!"

Exasperated, June exclaimed, "How did you know that? Were you pretending to be asleep? Did you hear what Dad just told me?"

"I heard him when he told us last night," he mumbled. "If you hadn't been daydreaming you'd have heard him too. Now go away and let me go back to sleep," he continued as he buried his head under the pillow.

She had no choice but to go exploring on her own. Wandering through the grounds, she soon found herself standing on the bank of the river. Climbing on top of a weathered overturned boat, she sat and watched the water gently flow by.

After awhile Cecil joined her. "I wonder why anyone would leave a boat here like this," he said. After a hasty inspection, he had his answer. There were cracks and holes in the bottom and sides. "I guess we won't be going out in this," he stated.

Situated so close to the water, it soon became their favorite spot. Sometimes they would sit on it and cast their fishing lines into the river. Other times they would use it as a launching pad for skipping stones across the water.

Cecil was a much better fisherman than June, as she didn't want to touch the fishing worms or hurt the fish. "Girls," he muttered as he slipped a worm onto the hook. "You're going to have to learn to do this yourself. I'm not going to do it forever."

"That's okay with me," she replied. She would much rather sit, book in hand, in the shade of the trees with her back against the boat and lazily wile the afternoon away. She hadn't outgrown her fascination with the printed word. Her books transported her to places she'd never seen and introduced her to people she'd never met. They had gotten her through some rough times in her life. She would be lost without them.

It was a good thing they could find ways to entertain themselves. Their first day's exploration had shown them that all their neighbors were their parents' ages. There wasn't a child or teen-ager on the site. Polly found a way to ease this situation, at least for a short time by inviting her niece, Barbara Jean, to spend a couple weeks with them. The girls had met when the family had visited Polly's brother David, his wife, and Barbara Jean in Wilmington, Delaware.

Being the same age, the girls soon discovered they had a lot in common. They both had crushes on the same movie stars, loved to read, go to the movies, and had large collections of paper dolls. Barbara Jean resembled her mother, with her dark hair and eyes. Unlike her mother, though, her eyes peered through thick, rimless glasses. She hated having to wear them, but was almost blind without them.

The time of her visit went by quickly. Since Barbara Jean wasn't as squeamish a fisherman as June, she and Cecil would sit on the boat and fish for hours. Sometimes June joined them, if her brother could be coerced into baiting her hook. If not, she'd sit on the boat and talk to them. Other times the two girls would perch on the picnic table and have long serious conversations.

Barbara Jean's father and mother were the first members of Polly's family the Harmans had met. While most of Polly's family lived in Mississippi, David had migrated to Delaware a few months earlier. Tall and lanky, with red wavy hair, he reminded June of Joseph Cotton, one of her favorite movie stars. David had some serious health problems as a result of the dust he inhaled in his job as an engraver of marble and granite.

Prior to the visit, Polly had talked to them about him. "His last name isn't the same as mine. It's Hardin. Both my mother and father were married before and had children. Mamma's first husband was a preacher. In fact he was the preacher who married Daddy and his first wife. Mamma and her first husband had David and my sister Ruby. Daddy and his first wife had a little boy, my brother Cecil."

"Mamma's husband and Daddy's wife died at about the same time. Daddy is very capable and protective of women, pretty much what you would expect from a southern gentlemen, and Mamma is one of the most helpless women you'd ever meet. Being neighbors with Daddy, she would call on him when she ran into a problem. She was impressed with his strength, and he liked having someone who needed him. Besides, they were both having trouble trying to raise children alone. Even though Mamma is ten years older than Daddy, they found they loved and needed each other, so they got married."

She grinned as she added, "Nine months from their wedding night my brother Fred was born. Five years later, I came along. Daddy always says that in our family we have hers, mine, and ours, but he always treated all of us as his."

She appeared to be lost in thought for a while before continuing, "Mamma said that when I made my entrance into the world, I only weighed a little over two pounds. The black woman who was with her when I was born put me inside her dress next to her breasts to keep me warm. Then she wrapped me in a blanket and put me in a basket on the opened door of the oven. Daddy always said that he thought that was what kept me alive."

She filled their lemonade glasses before she said, "I was named Clara Louise after my Aunt Clara. Right from the beginning, Daddy said I didn't seem like a Clara, and he started calling me his Polly Wally-Wampus Cat. After awhile, this got shortened to Polly, and that's what I've been called ever since. Sometimes Daddy still calls me his Wampus Cat, but I won't let anyone else call me that."

June silently let the words "Wampus Cat" roll around on her tongue, but one look at Polly's red hair, and remembering the temper that went with it, made her think it wouldn't be wise to voice them.

She and Cecil had recently been the objects of that temper. They'd been bickering, more to amuse themselves than for any other reason. When she'd told them to stop, they'd quit momentarily, only to pick it up later.

"I told you to stop that!" Polly told them one more time. "I'm trying to cook this fish you caught. If you don't cut it out, that's all she wrote. There'll be no fish for supper."

"Aw, Mom we're just kidding around," June said. She had barely finished speaking when Polly, her eyes blazing, red-hair flying flashed by carrying the skillet full of hot fish.

"You may be kidding, but I'm not," she said, as she flung the skillet out the door. They stood, astonished as the fish flew in all directions. "Now, you can tell your dad why you don't have any supper," she said, walking out the door and slamming it behind her.

"Boy, we really did it that time," Cecil said. When their dad got home he found them in the yard, surrounded by the neighbors' cats. They were trying to clean up the mess. That night they dined on bologna sandwiches, but no one opened their mouths to complain.

～

Over the next couple months they felt like vagabonds, moving three more times before school started. The first move took place while June was visiting her cousins Bonnie and Ruby in their new home in Pennsylvania. When she left home to board a bus in Washington to go visit her cousins in Harrisburg, her home was still at The Bush River Inn. When she returned two weeks later, it was to a new court in Harve de Grace, Maryland. Burrel had transferred to another job, and they'd again moved to be close to his work.

Not having been part of this new move, it took her awhile to get used to the unfamiliar outdoor surroundings. With everything inside the trailer being the same, she almost felt she should be able to step outside and walk along the Susquehanna River or relax by the old boat.

They were now living near Harve de Grace, a town famous for its horse racing track. Though they'd heard of it, the family didn't live there long enough to visit it. They probably wouldn't have anyway since neither Burrel nor Polly were the least interested in this sport. Nor did the gambling aspect appeal to them. Burrel had never tried it and Polly, like June and Cecil, while in Zanesville, had tested her luck with the slot machines. Although she hadn't told anyone, her experience had been as disastrous as June and Cecil's.

A few weeks before school started, they moved again, this time to Perrysville, Maryland. Burrel had tried to find a trailer park, but there were none close to his job. With so many military wives and defense workers moving into the area, housing, or in their case, a place to park their home, was non-existent. He had to settle for a spot next to a gas station. While the solution wasn't the most desirable, it did allow the family to stay together. One advantage was its proximity to the high school. It was so close, June could look out her bedroom window into its front door.

She and Cecil had spent most of the summer in each other's and Polly's company. They were beginning to get a little bored and anxious for school to start, so they could meet people their own age. As it turned out, they were never to step foot in that schoolhouse. The day before school started, Burrel came home with the news that they were moving again. Even though his current job wouldn't end for a couple months, he had the opportunity to go on to one that was just beginning in what was then called Cedar Point, Maryland. Years later, as a young newlywed sailor, Cecil was to be stationed there as an air traffic control operator. By then the base was known as the Patuxent River Naval Air Station.

"If I take this job now, the kids won't be starting one school now and having to change in a couple months," he told them that evening. "I know you kids have been expecting to go to that school," he said, nodding toward the one across the street. "But you wouldn't want to have to change again, would you?"

"Dad," June reassured him, "It doesn't matter where we go to school. We'll have to get acquainted with new kids, wherever we go. I just don't want to have to do it twice." She cringed at the very thought of again being the new girl in the class. "If only I could look at it the way Dad does," she thought. "Maybe someday when I'm older, I will be able to see it his way." Deep in her heart, though, she didn't think she ever would.

CHAPTER FIVE

THE TIE THAT BINDS

They were planning to move in a few days, but before they did, their life, as they knew it, almost collapsed around them.

Trouble was brewing between their father and Polly. June and Cecil weren't sure what was going on, just that things were beginning to change. Their first inkling was when Polly spent a week with her brother David's family in Delaware. She told them she needed some time away.

"Away? Away from what?" June wondered. This sounded all too familiar to her. Noticing her distress, Polly assured her she would be back, and true to her word, she did return.

The night she came home she and Burrel talked into the wee hours of the morning. "It's time we made this permanent," Polly said. "I know we couldn't get married before because of the problems with your divorce, but that's no longer the case. You keep saying you want to marry me, but action speaks louder than words."

Her flushed cheeks and the glint of tears in her eyes clearly illustrated her anger and the depth of her pain. Burrel, who didn't like this kind of confrontation, tried to placate her. "Polly, you know I love you, and I want to marry you, but why does it have to be now?" He didn't want to voice his true feelings, but he was afraid of the commitment. Living with her, these months, he was aware of her many sterling qualities, not the least being the way she had helped the children.

On the other hand the temper that went with her red hair was another matter. He wanted his home life to be calm and tranquil and knew this wouldn't be the case with this tempestuous woman. He wasn't sure he could deal with a lifetime of it.

Because of what had happened in the last couple years, he was torn between his love for this woman and his fear of failing again. His divorce from Priscilla had left its scars on him and June and Cecil. These months of being with Polly was helping to heal them.

His thoughts were interrupted by the sound of Polly's voice, "I guess we should have waited until we could get married, but when I went back to West Virginia and saw how unhappy June was, I couldn't stand it. She wanted a home of her own, but more than that, she wanted her daddy. I knew you couldn't bring the kids with you, without someone to take care of them. I guess I fell in love, as much with them, as I did with you."

Listening intently, Burrel was moved by what she was saying, and he knew every word was true. "I know I talked you into us living together, because I couldn't stand to think of how unhappy the children were," she said. "They needed a home and to be with their father right then! I was willing to wait to get married, but I'm not going to wait any longer."

"They still need you," he exclaimed. "And so do I." Her spirits soared, momentarily. Then sank again as she realized he still hadn't said he'd marry her.

"I'm going home to Mississippi tomorrow. If you don't love me enough to marry me now, you never will. I know you don't like my temper, and I can promise to try to change, but I'm afraid it's as much a part of me as my red hair. Why do you think Daddy called me his wampus cat? Mamma always said a wampus was a wild cat."

"I can believe it!" Burrel said, trying to tease and humor her out of her mood, but she was having none of it. "I'll tell the kids tomorrow," she sadly sighed before turning her back and pretending to fall asleep. Although he followed her example, lying beside her, he silently reflected on what she'd said.

Then, unbidden, images raced across his mind, of Polly when he'd first met her in Baltimore, of her flight from Tony Torintino, and of her reaction the first time she'd met June. When he first brought Polly to West Virginia to his sister's farm where June was staying, June had come running down the hill with outstretched arms to hug him. Polly, a total stranger, had stepped between them and embraced June in her arms. What a welcome for a lonely little girl.

Remembering how, little more than a kid herself, Polly had made a home for them. He smiled when he remembered her struggle to learn to cook and to sew. He couldn't erase the picture of her struggling over the first dress she'd made for June. Since his daughter thought Polly could do everything, she hadn't wanted her to know she didn't know how to sew.

Then, unbidden, other images intruded, of the night he'd returned to Petersburg and found his family gone, and of the looks on June and Cecil's faces when he'd told them their mother wasn't coming back. He remembered when he and Priscilla had gotten married that he had never once thought it wouldn't last.

He knew, now, he'd failed in that marriage even though they'd seemed to have everything going for them. A failure once, how could he expect this marriage to work? Polly was so young; she still thought everything was possible if you just wanted it enough. These last few years had taught him that life doesn't always work out that way.

As the first light of dawn inched its way into the room, and he finally drifted off to sleep, he was still wavering. Should he or shouldn't he? Would the strong love he felt for her overcome his fear of failure? He knew if he married her with the difference in their ages and temperaments, life wouldn't always be smooth sailing.

Would he be able to handle it? He had married the first time with such high hopes. Now he felt much older, wiser, and decidedly more frightened.

The next morning, standing by the table, pouring steaming coffee into his cup, he was tired and didn't feel prepared to handle hearing Polly tell June and Cecil she was leaving. "I'm homesick for my parents and am going home to Mississippi," she said. "I haven't seen them for over a year now. I'm calling Daddy this morning and leaving this afternoon."

The look on June's face mirrored her fear as she asked, "How long are you going to be gone?" This scene was reminiscent of what had happened when her other mother left. Her voice sounded anxious, barely above a whisper when she implored, "You're coming back, aren't you?"

"I don't know," Polly replied, first looking at June, then turning her attention to Burrel. "That's up to your dad." June looked to him for reassurance, but with his somber eyes on Polly's face, he didn't notice his daughter's beseeching look.

Feeling her world again crumbling under her feet, June felt like screaming, "There's no place to be alone in this darn trailer. I've got to get out of here!" Action followed the thought as she ran through the doorway and across the street to the school grounds. Sitting on the grass beneath a large maple tree, tears flowing down her cheeks, she buried her face in her folded arms and remained there until she felt a light touch on her shoulder.

"There's nothing to cry about," Polly said. "I'm not going anywhere, except to my wedding. You'd better come on home and get into your best bib and tucker. You and Cecil are going to stand up with us."

"Do you mean you're not going to Mississippi?" June asked, anxiously. "You're not going to change your mind, are you?"

"Oh, we'll go to Mississippi, some day, but we'll go as a family. I want Mamma and Daddy to meet my husband and my son and daughter. I can't wait to show you all off."

Holding hands, they walked side-by-side back to the trailer and the reluctant bridegroom. Hearing her tell the kids that she was going home had made him realize he was really going to lose her. "This will never do," he thought, right before he blurted out the words she'd been waiting to hear. "You can't leave. We're going to get married today."

~

Then a little later that morning the four of them trooped into the courthouse in a neighboring county for the license. That afternoon found them standing before the preacher, reciting their vows. Although June and Cecil weren't old enough to be official witnesses, Polly insisted they be allowed to stand at their side, while the witnesses stood behind them. "I'm not just marrying your father," she said. "I'm marrying all three of you." After looking up into Burrel's face and repeating, "Until death do we part," she turned toward June and Cecil and whispered, "You, too." This was a promise she was to keep.

Following the ceremony, the four of them went to a nearby restaurant for a celebration dinner. Other diners noticed the festive foursome, the pretty redheaded woman in her sky blue crepe dress, the handsome blonde man in the dark blue suit and the boy and girl, so close in size they could be mistaken for twins. As waiters and patrons observed them, they wondered about the occasion. "Nobody would ever guess, we just got married," June said.

"We sure did!" Polly exclaimed, emphasizing the "We".

"No one will believe Cecil and I went to our parents' wedding!" June exclaimed. "I can't wait to tell Molly," she continued, referring to the one girl she'd met in Perrysville.

Burrel and Polly exchanged glances before Polly said, "It might be better if this is our own little secret. You may not have noticed, but most people we've met have just taken it for granted we were already married. They also believe I'm your real mother. I think we'd better keep it that way."

Burrel nodded his agreement while Cecil gave his sister a withering stare and muttered, "Don't you know anything?" He didn't add, "You Baby," but June could imagine him saying it.

She flushed, then giggled, then flushed even more when their serious faces became wreathed in laughter. "I wasn't even thinking," June said. "I'll never tell anyone. Not unless you tell me it's alright to do so," she solemnly promised.

"Hursh this serious talk," Burrel said. "This is a happy day! We're truly a family now. Let's celebrate!" As he raised his glass in the air and said, "To us!" they clinked theirs together and enthusiastically joined him in the toast.

Neighbors may have wondered about the occasion when they heard the happy foursome return a few hours later, but no one had the chance to ask. The next day the family again moved, starting their new life in Great Mills. People meeting them for the first time may have wondered about the youth of the mother, but no one ever questioned it.

CHAPTER SIX

LIFE IN THE JUNKYARD

As they traveled from Perrysville to Great Mills, they left the sights and sounds of the city to find themselves surrounded by woods and gently rolling hills. The pine trees lining the highway reminded Polly of her home in Mississippi, while the deep woods and occasional field made June think of her home by the cavern. Relaxed and happy, they weren't prepared for the sight that greeted them when Burrel pulled the trailer alongside a long narrow building that housed a hodgepodge of businesses.

The barbershop, sporting goods store, small grocery, and combination real estate office and used car dealership were overshadowed by the sights and sounds coming from the tavern. Men in work clothes were coming and going, shouting colorful greetings to each other. They could hear loud strains of "Chattanooga Choo Choo" coming from the jukebox each time the door was opened.

"Well, here we are," Burrel said. "We're home!" Three faces stared incredulously at him. He must be joking! Then spotting the other trailers parked behind the building and the regulation washhouse, they knew he was serious. This was going to be their new residence. It didn't bother Cecil, but June and Polly both felt their hearts sink.

"I'm sorry. I know this isn't much, but it was the best I could do," Burrel explained. If he'd known, though, what his wife and daughter would soon encounter here, he wouldn't have stayed one minute longer.

Unaware of the danger he was exposing them to, he continued, "This place has become a boomtown. Before they started building the base, it was just a farming community. Hundreds of families have moved in to work on the base, and there's just no place to put them. One guy owns all these businesses and he is getting rich. He's gouging everyone with his prices, but there aren't very many other places to go."

Polly felt her temper rise at the thought of someone taking advantage of the defense construction workers, but before she could voice her anger, Burrel silenced her with his slow smile and a gentle pat on the hand. "I'm afraid this goes with the territory. If we're all going to be together, we'll have to put up with it for a while. Once we have a chance to look around, I'm sure I'll be able to find something better."

"I don't think anything could be worse," Polly muttered, only to realize when Burrel drove into their designated spot, it not only could be, but was. "Good Lord!" she exclaimed. "It's a junkyard!"

She looked in horror at the dozen or more cars in all stages of disrepair, parked haphazardly around the grounds. Situated among them were an equal number of trailers. All around was evidence that the residents had tried to make a home in the midst of this metal jungle. Patches of grass could be seen peeking through the clumps of dirt in the minuscule yards. Flowers were growing along the concrete patios and spilling out of brightly colored pots and makeshift window boxes. In the only space devoid of trailers or junk cars someone had erected a swing set and improvised a sandbox from a truck tire.

Neighbors were milling about and children were running and playing. A couple of the men ambled over to where Burrel was setting up the trailer. A few minutes later Polly noticed they were hunched down helping him. With three pairs of busy hands, the work was quickly completed, and the family was again settled in their home.

Before the sun set they had met most of their neighbors. All the men, like Burrel, were construction workers at the Cedar Point Sea Plane Base. He had worked with some of them on other defense construction sites, and Polly had already met a couple of the women. These construction gypsies were a new breed of people. Most were young couples with children, living in trailers. Like Burrel, they'd found this to be the only way to keep the family together. Many were far from their roots, but like the Harmans, were at home wherever they set up their trailer.

Small touches, like the flowers planted around the patios, crisp brightly colored curtains, or family pictures on the wall were evidence of the women's efforts to make their surroundings homelike. June and Cecil had leisurely explored the area. They hadn't found anything that interested them nor had they found anyone close to their own age. "Oh, well," June thought, "Maybe I'll meet some girls I like at school tomorrow."

~

Their first morning was hectic as Burrel hurried to get ready for work and June and Cecil for school. "There's my ride," Burrel said as one of the men he'd met the day before drove up and stopped outside their door. Kissing Polly and waving goodbye to June and Cecil, he was quickly out the door and on his way to his first day on the new job. As the car disappeared from her sight, Polly was thinking that Burrel being able to car pool would help them save their gasoline rationing stamps and maybe allow them to take a trip to West Virginia to see Burrel's father, Pap. On Burrel's last job he'd had to use most of his stamps to get to and from work and it had been months since they'd seen Burrel's father and his brothers and sisters.

Rationing was new. Getting accustomed to it wasn't easy. A ration board had been established shortly after the war started. So far, gasoline, tires, shoes, and some food products were rationed. The board issued ration stamps to all families for these scarce items. A short time before, during the depression, there hadn't been enough money to buy what you needed. Now that people were making more money, some of the products weren't available. In cases where they were, women found they didn't have enough ration stamps to get what they wanted.

June wasn't thinking about such mundane things, as she and Cecil joined the others at the school bus stop. She was both nervous and excited about starting in a new school. In her dreams the night before, she was standing in front of the class being introduced as the new student. As the teacher said her name, everyone pointed to her feet and started laughing. She'd looked down and found she was wearing her house slippers.

When she'd told Polly about it, she'd said, "You're just nervous about going to a new school. Don't worry about it. Everything will be okay. I'm sure you'll meet some girls you like." Then laughing she added, "Just to be on the safe side, I'll check your feet before you go out the door."

This time, though, with all the defense construction workers moving into the area, June and Cecil weren't the only new kids in the class. Since there were so many, they were spared the agony of standing in front of the class with all eyes boring into them. Instead, everyone was assigned a seat, and then the students took turns introducing themselves.

As June's eyes scanned the room, they settled first on a short stocky girl with short curly hair, then on a taller one in a smooth pageboy. They both looked familiar. As June continued to look at them and wonder where she'd seen them before, her eyes first met one girl's eyes then the other's. They both smiled and gave a little wave. Listening intently for their names, as they introduced themselves, she heard first Nadia then Joy. They were the girls she'd met the one-day she and Cecil had attended the school in Beltsville.

"This is great," she thought. Her dad had told her they would be crossing paths with people they'd met in other schools, but she was, nevertheless, surprised to see them. They were soon to become her best friends.

She and Cecil had never attended a school quite like this one. Located miles from any town, it was a low white clapboard building. Sunlight streamed through the many multi-paned windows, making it unnecessary to turn on the lights except on the dreariest of days.

Two women, sisters, were the administrators and also taught some classes. The students were told to call the one Miss Phoebe and the other Miss Jane. Both were imposing, tall and stately, dressed in black skirts and white high collared blouses. They wore prim hairstyles and black, chunky heeled, sensible shoes. Everything about these women seemed to proclaim, "No nonsense."

When Miss Phoebe introduced herself, June stared at her glasses. Like none she'd ever seen, they weren't held in place with sidepieces fitting over the ears. Instead Miss Phoebe's seemed to perch on her nose with no apparent means of support. Hanging from the wire frame on the left side was a black grosgrain ribbon. It didn't seem to serve any purpose. "It must be a decoration," June thought. She remembered seeing an actor wear something similar, in a movie, but his had only had one lens. Smiling introspectively, she remembered her dad saying she should keep her eyes and ears open. There was always something new to learn. She had a feeling, this time, he was going to be right. If nothing else, she was going to learn what kept those glasses on Miss Phoebe's nose.

~

For the girls this was almost like a finishing school. Miss Phoebe taught them the finer points of the social graces. One thing she told them was, "When in doubt about the right thing to do, remember kindness is what counts. Always make the other person feel comfortable." This reminded June of things her mother had taught her when she was a little girl.

Miss Jane fueled June's interest in interior decorating, one she never outgrew. The course title was Related Science. In this class they learned about color, style, balance, design, and the different styles of architecture. "Women set the tone in a home," Miss Jane would say. "Everyone around you will feel better in a gracious setting. Whether you are a wife and mother or a career woman, you'll have a home. Make it one that expresses the real you."

The sisters encouraged creativity in their students. For June this meant writing. Miss Phoebe would say, "If you want to write, you need to read. Read, it's a way to travel all over the world. Whether you read fiction or nonfiction, a book is a great teacher. You'll be surprised how much you can learn between those pages."

No one thought that this teaching was out of place in this rural schoolhouse bulging at the seams with a mixture of farmers and construction workers' children. These two women were born teachers and instilled in many of their students a love of learning and an appreciation for the finer things in life. The girls soon learned their teachers' austere appearance contradicted their softer, gentler natures. June marveled at how much their teachings reflected that of her own parents.

Some of her happiest days were spent in this school. Her new friends, Nadia and Joy and Miss Phoebe and Miss Jane weren't the only reasons for her enthusiasm. In the seat across the aisle was a dark haired boy with eyes the color of turquoise. With his tan skin he looked like he'd spent the summer in the sun. She was to find later that his coloring was more the result of his Spanish heritage than any time he might have spent at the beach.

Nadia, Joy and June all had their eyes on him, but June was the one he liked. He always saved a seat for her next to him on the bus and waited for her after class so they could have lunch together.

Noticing them walking together through the school grounds or sitting on the steps talking during recess, Cecil enjoyed teasing her about having a boyfriend. This spilled over into their home life, bringing about a dinner table discussion.

"Who is this little boy Cecil is talking about?" Polly asked. "Does his dad work at the base or is he a local?"

Highly indignant, June replied, "Mom, he's not a little boy. He's thirteen years old! I'd hardly call that a little boy!"

"I don't think anyone's noticed, but our little girl is growing up," Burrel said. His smile caused his eyes to sparkle as he looked at his daughter.

"I'll be thirteen in four months," June proudly exclaimed. "He's just a boy I talk to at school. His dad works with you, Dad," she continued. Wanting to maintain her privacy she added, "We're just friends. He talks to me about how much he hated to leave his home in Baltimore, and I tell him about some of the places we've lived."

Grinning, Cecil said, "The way you two have your heads together, I'd say he's your boyfriend!" As June's cheeks flushed, he continued to tease her until her temper flared.

"You should talk! How about all the girls who are always plopping down beside you at lunch? You should see them, Mom. They jostle each other to see who's going to sit beside him. They've got him thinking he's a movie star or something."

"That's better than mooning around all the time like you and Ramon do," he said. Their parents had been looking first at one than at the other. Burrel was amused, it reminded him of the times he'd teased his sisters, but he could see that June was getting upset. With his two words that always stopped any argument in its tracks, he proclaimed, "Hursh i-med-e-ate-ly!"

June and Cecil exchanged glances and as always, when they heard those words from him, they immediately "hurshed". No one had ever tested him to see what would happen if they didn't.

Ramon also liked to talk about his record collection. He was a fan of the big band sound, with Glen Miller and his orchestra being his favorite. He told June he'd loan her some of his records, but she had to decline since the Harman's didn't have a record player. Talking about all the big bands made him sound hep. Having to admit she didn't have any way to play his records made her feel like a real square.

~

From their patio they could hear the sounds of music emanating from the open door of the tavern. June wanted to go closer so she could hear better, but Polly wouldn't let her. "I won't let you go by yourself, but if you and Cecil want to have a coke and listen to some music, I'll go with you. Your dad won't be home for a while. We should be able to listen to a few records."

All eyes turned to look at them when they walked through the door. A burly looking redheaded man, wearing a shirt with "Tom" stitched across the pocket, whistled at Polly. She ignored him as she sat down with June and Cecil and started feeding nickels into the jukebox. They tapped their feet to the beat as the strains of Chattanooga Choo Choo and Elmer's Tune filled the room. June dreamily listened to Ray Eberely softly sing the first chorus of "Tangerine", then grinned as Helen O'Connell swung into her lively rendition of the second chorus.

At dinner that night, Polly said to Burrel, "Remember in Zanesville when I told you I'd taken the kids to a Honkey Tonk, and it was only a movie?"

Grinning, he replied, "Yes, I remember. You were trying to pull a joke on me, and I didn't even know what a Honkey Tonk was. What made you think about that now?" he asked.

"Well, today I did take them to a Honky Tonk." At his raised eyebrow, she quickly continued. "Ramon has been talking about his big band records, and June isn't familiar with them. She was trying to hear the jukebox from the tavern. From here you can't hear very well, so I took them up there, and we listened to the music."

"You took the kids to a beer joint?" he exploded. "Woman, don't you have any sense? That's not a fit place for kids their age."

"Neither is living in a junkyard!" Polly stormily replied. "And I don't hear you complaining about that." Her cheeks flushed with anger as she continued, "There's no decent place around here for them to go. I shouldn't have to take them to a tavern to listen to music. They should be going to soda shops with their friends."

This was the first she'd complained about the way they had to live. Immediately contrite, he said, "Polly, I know it isn't easy for any of you living like we do, but it's the only way we can be together. I thought you felt the way I do about it."

"I do," Polly replied. "I just lost my temper. I don't care where we have to live, just so the four of us can be together. The tavern isn't really bad. In fact, while we were there a couple families came in for dinner."

"The food looked pretty good, Dad." Cecil said. "This one kid had a big hamburger and French fries. I wouldn't mind having one of those myself one of these days."

This came as no surprise to anyone. Everyone was aware of his love of food. The family liked to tease him about it. Polly had told him that if he'd been Chinese, his name would have been "One Long Gut." In response, Burrel had said he didn't think it mattered to Cecil what he was called as long as he was called for dinner.

"Tomorrow is Saturday and for once I don't have to work. If you want to, we can go up there for lunch. How does that sound to you?" he asked. He got no arguments from any of them.

Getting ready for bed, June could smell tobacco smoke wafting its way through her open window. Looking out, she saw the red glow of her dad's cigarette as he sat smoking on the patio. Slipping out the door, she moved to his side and quietly said, "Dad, I don't care where we live. This place is alright."

He could feel a catch in his throat as he looked at his daughter's anxious blue eyes. "She must really have been miserable without me or her mother if she thought this place was alright," he thought.

"This war won't last forever," he said. "Maybe once it's over, we can settle down somewhere. If I had my way, I'd like to go back home to

West Virginia and find another cave to manage. Would you like that?" he asked.

"If that's what you want, it would be alright with me, but I really like living in Maryland. I love my new school, but I really don't care where we live as long as you, Mom, and Cecil are here."

Looking at her serious face, he wondered what he and her mother had done to this child. As she had reminded them, she was almost a teenager, but she sounded like an adult.

These last couple years seemed to have robbed her of her childhood. He realized that she and Cecil had been forced to carry burdens beyond their years. Had he made a mistake not taking them with him as soon as he found out their mother was gone? He had tried to do what he thought was best for them, now he wasn't sure he'd done the right thing.

After she said goodnight and returned to the trailer, he continued to sit, smoking, and thinking. Meeting and marrying Polly was the best thing he'd done for his children and for himself. Things didn't always go smoothly between them, but he was thankful she'd come along when she did.

～

When they went to the tavern for lunch the next day, Burrel found himself agreeing with Polly. He wouldn't want June and Cecil to go there alone, but it would be all right as long as one or both of their parents could be with them.

The few times they were there, they not only listened to the music, but to the people around them. They soon discovered this was a home away from home for several of the "regulars". These men were married, with families, but as they confided in anyone who would listen, their wives thought it would be an embarrassment to live, as one lonely man said, "Like vagabonds, going from place to place in a trailer."

Hearing this complaint, Polly couldn't keep quiet. "You can tell your wife for me that there's nothing embarrassing about going with your man. I'd be here, even if we had to live in a tent. She should come and visit, and see how these women are making homes for their families."

"Unfortunately, not all women are alike," he responded. "My wife says staying in our hometown is a way to give stability to our children. It might be alright for them, but it's mighty lonely for me."

June observed, a few weeks later, this same man sitting in a booth with a pretty young blonde woman. At first she thought his wife had joined him until she overheard some of the men talking about his wife having made a mistake staying at home. She thought about the wife and children back in their hometown and wondered what was going to happen. Her curiosity was never satisfied, as she never saw the man or the blonde again.

Several times they had seen Mr. Overby, the owner of the tavern, and his three sons either in the tavern, on the grounds walking around the junk cars, or in one of their other businesses. All four of them were big unpleasant looking men with heavy jowls, broad shoulders, thick chests and large bellies that lapped over their belts. Even though they owned a barbershop, from the looks of their greasy unkempt hair, none of them took advantage of its services.

The expression in their eyes was cruel. June had overheard Mr. Overby tell one of his customers who'd complained about his prices, "If you don't like the way I run my business, you can get the hell out. I don't need your business, and I don't care if you want to drive the extra ten miles to town to do your shopping."

She'd also noticed the way he and his sons looked at Polly and were beginning to look at her. One thing she knew was that she wouldn't want to be alone with any of them.

One Saturday, while Burrel and the other men in the trailer court were working, and Cecil had spent the night with a classmate something happened that reinforced the dislike and fear June had for the four Overbys. She and Polly were sitting on the patio enjoying the Indian summer day when they heard angry voices coming from the vicinity of the playground. "What in the world is going on?" Polly said as she stood and glanced in the direction of the sound. June looked, too, then replied, "I can't see anything. Let's go see."

Other women and children joined them as they rushed toward the playground. The sight confronting them was one June was never to forget. A handsome, slender young man, his dark hair falling onto his forehead, his brown eyes filled with fear and pain was screaming, "Let me go!" as two of Mr. Overby's sons held his arms behind his back, while their father and other brother hit him in the face and stomach.

As he writhed in pain, and continued to cry out, June looked around at the adults, expecting them to put a stop to it. The only man in the group was home today because he was recuperating from surgery. The women looked sickened and frightened. "Stop it, Mom. Make them stop," she cried.

"I can't," Polly said.

Until this minute June had thought Polly could do anything. She couldn't believe she'd heard those two words. As they echoed in her mind she screamed at the men, "Stop it! You're killing him!"

"Mind your own business," Mr. Overby snarled. "This is what happens to people who try to get out of paying their bills!" As he spoke, the young man sagged forward and the Overbys, father and son, kicked him in his head and stomach.

The crunching sound as their boots connected with his head was more than June could bear. Lunging toward them, she screamed, "Stop it! Stop it!" Before she reached them, Polly and one of the neighbors grabbed her and held her back. Whispering, Polly told her someone had called the police.

She could hear sirens wailing, first in the distance, then drawing closer and closer, until with lights flashing, two state highway patrol cars stopped a few feet from where she was standing.

The Overbys had let go of the young man and merged into the crowd. Their victim was lying limp and unconscious on the ground. "Who saw what happened?" the younger trooper inquired. Hearing no response, he looked around at the horrified group. Knowing these men as he did, he didn't have to be told what had happened.

It was well known at the police barracks that they ran a loan shark business. Once they got their hooks into someone by loaning him money, that person soon found himself buried in debt. What started as a hundred dollar loan could soon become a thousand dollar debt as the interest accelerated.

The young trooper was aware this wasn't the first victim they'd decided to teach a lesson. He knew some of his fellow officers had been paid to look the other way, but he had turned down their offer of a bribe. This time he was certain he had them. Surely, someone in this group would speak up. If so he'd be able to put this vermin away for a long time.

"We all saw it. It was the Overbys," a female voice declared. Turning toward the voice, he saw it had come from a young girl, barely in her teens. Her tear stained face reflected the horror of what she'd seen, but she looked as determined as he was that these men weren't going to get away with it.

Unfortunately, he was going to need some adults to testify. "I saw it!" a redheaded young woman said. "My daughter is right. It was the Overbys."

"That's right. It was the Overbys," the lone male witness proclaimed. He was joined by a chorus of voices agreeing with what the others had said.

"That does it, boys," the trooper said to the smirking Overbys. "Lean against the car and spread your legs." He and his partner quickly frisked and cuffed them before shoving them into the cruiser.

As the car sped away, the little group slowly walked back to their homes. "What could we have done?" they asked each other. While, deep in their hearts they knew they were no match for these brutal men, they felt shame that this girl had expected so much more than they were able to deliver.

When Burrel arrived home from work, he could tell by June and Polly's faces that something was wrong. When he asked and was told what had happened, he knew one of Polly's fears had been realized. She had often commented that June thought she could walk on water, and she didn't know what would happen when she found out she was a mortal, like everyone else. Today, she'd found out.

"I hope she'll get over her disappointment in me," she told him. "You should have seen those men. They were like vicious animals. If anyone had tried to interfere they'd have been hurt, hurt bad. June was so horrified at what those men were doing that she didn't feel fear, like the rest of us did. I hope she'll come to understand. We did the best we could, by calling the police."

"Are you going to testify?" he asked. When she nodded affirmatively, he said, "They'll be out on bail. We'd better find another place to live. Tomorrow, we'll go out and look around."

CHAPTER SEVEN

WINTER IN MARYLAND

The place they found was a beautiful spot in the country beside a farmhouse. The farmer had set up a place to rent for one trailer. This was a beautiful setting, much more pleasant than where they had been living. On one side of their parking place was the farmhouse. Behind it were fields, lying fallow now, but in Burrel's mind's eye he could picture them lush with growing crops in coming seasons.

The wooded area across the road immediately caught June and Cecil's attention. They could hardly wait to begin exploring. Watching their excited faces, Burrel said, "I don't think we need to look any further. I think we've found our new home." By evening they had moved in.

The following Saturday, June and Cecil explored the woods. This soon became a favorite spot for them. After crossing the road and climbing an embankment, they found themselves surrounded by tall trees, growing so close together that very little sun managed to creep past the bare branches.

As they wandered deeper into the woods, the only sound they could hear was the crunch of their footsteps on the carpet of gold, brown and crimson leaves. The clumps of holly added touches of red and green to the landscape. "We'll have to come back and get some of this for Christmas," June said.

A few minutes later, they found a deep ravine. "Let's see what's down there," Cecil suggested. Before June could respond, he was scrambling down the steep incline, grabbing onto branches to slow his rapid decent. Following his lead, June made her way more cautiously, not letting go of one tree until she had her hand securely on the next one.

Cecil laughed at her slow progress. "Let go. You're not going to fall," he yelled. Not wanting him to think she was scared, she released her hold on the tree and took a few cautious steps down the hill.

"Hey, this is okay," she yelled, as she ran the rest of the way. At the end of her mad dash, she found herself tumbling the last few steps, landing in a pile of leaves at the bottom of the ravine. Standing up and brushing them from her clothing and hair she said, "That was fun. I bet you can't do that!"

Cecil had found something he thought would be even more exciting. At the top of the ravine were thick vines hanging from the trees. "After we look around down here, let's see if those vines will hold us."

"Who do you think you are, Tarzan?" she asked. "Just because we just saw Tarzan and Jane in a movie doesn't mean we have to act like them," she added. In response to his challenging look, she tossed her head and with a look of determination said, "If you can do it, so can I."

Before the afternoon was over, they'd found sturdy vines and firmly gripping them with both hands they found themselves airborne. Their imitation Tarzan yells as they swung from the trees, sent birds flying and little animals scurrying for safety. When they got home, Polly had hot chocolate ready for them. "It was fun, Mom," Cecil said. She listened with a measure of trepidation as they talked about their escapades. She was concerned about them swinging from vines and going to the bottom of a ravine, but they seemed to know how to take care of themselves.

No matter what their environment, they seemed to adapt. When they'd lived close to the city they'd spent their Saturdays at the Smithsonian or at a downtown movie house. They seemed equally happy here exploring the woods. "I guess, since we're going to be vagabonds," she thought, "It's a good thing they can change with the territory."

Much to June's relief, they still rode the same school bus. Only now they were on it longer, giving her more time to sit next to Ramon. He was talking about having her come home with him some evening after school so she could hear his record collection. She wouldn't be able to do it until she could be sure her dad wouldn't be working overtime and could give her a ride home.

~

Polly didn't know how to drive, and this incident reinforced her feeling that she needed to learn. "These kids have places they would like to go. If I could drive, I could take them. It would also save you the trouble of having to take me to the grocery store on Saturdays. You work such long hours you need some time just to relax when you have a few hours off."

"You don't have to sell me on the idea," he said. "I think you definitely need to learn. We'll go into Leonardtown on Saturday and you can get a permit. I'll take you out to practice every chance I get."

Her first time behind the wheel, Burrel sat beside her while June and Cecil sat in the backseat. The car bucked and swayed as she started down the driveway. "To your right!" Burrel yelled, when she swerved left toward the gatepost. "That's better," he said, encouragingly, as she turned the wheel and narrowly missed the post.

June and Cecil exchanged worried glances as their dad guided her through the rudiments of maneuvering the car over hills and around curves. A few heated words were exchanged in the front seat as Polly became frustrated from all the instructions he was giving her. "Why don't you be quiet and let me drive?" she muttered.

"If I did that you'd have us wrapped around a telephone pole by now!" he responded. Then in more soothing tones, he continued, "You're not doing anything different from what all new drivers do. It just takes time and patience. You'll learn."

"Time, I have. Patience, I don't," she grumbled. "Light me a cigarette, will you?" she added. "It'll calm my nerves." As he lit it and handed it to her, she took her eyes off the road and one hand off the steering wheel. It was only for a second, but that was long enough to cause the car to veer toward the side of the road. Seeing them heading for the embankment, Cecil yelled, "Dad, she's going to kill us!"

Grabbing the wheel, Burrel quickly had everything under control. "I'll never learn," Polly cried. "If you'll tell me how to stop this darn thing, I'll let you take over."

She wasn't the only one glad the first lesson was over. The backseat passengers were visibility relieved. "I think I'll stay home the next time, Mom," Cecil said. June agreed with him. She would, too.

The next few lessons took place on the farm. Burrel waited until she had picked up the basics of operating the vehicle before letting her take to the highway again. After a few weeks June and Cecil were asked to go along and much to their surprise and relief she had become a good driver.

When they returned home, Polly told June, "If you wait until you get married to learn to drive, I'd advise you not to let your husband teach you. If it had taken me much longer to learn, I'm not sure the marriage would have survived."

To June's look of dismay, Polly responded, "I'm only kidding. Your dad was probably a better teacher than I would have been. He only got mad when he thought our lives were in danger."

Burrel grinned as he teasingly said, "I'd say that was about every five minutes." Remembering their experience as passengers, June and Cecil were inclined to agree with him.

~

A couple, the Morrisons, and their two daughters lived in the farmhouse. The girls had both graduated from high school and worked in Leonardtown. Merideth, the oldest, worked in the library, and since they shared an interest in books, she and June became friends despite the difference in their ages. Often she would bring a stack of books home to June. Now that winter had arrived Polly, June, and Cecil would spend most of their free time curled up with one of these books.

One Saturday Polly took them into Leonardtown to see a new movie, Holiday Inn, with Bing Crosby and Fred Astair. It was full of music and dancing. The best part, though, was a new song, I'm Dreaming of a White Christmas, sung by Bing Crosby. June had read in a movie magazine that Bing hadn't wanted to sing it. She couldn't imagine why as she listened to moviegoers hum it as they left the theater.

Looking out of her bedroom window, a few weeks before the big day, she didn't have to dream of a white Christmas. As far as her eyes could see, the landscape was enveloped in a blanket of white. Snow and ice coated all the tree branches and clung to the electric and telephone wires. This was truly a winter wonderland.

Polly had been listening to the radio and heard the announcement that the school superintendent was calling off school because the roads were slippery and considered hazardous.

For the first time in their lives June and Cecil got to stay home from school because of the weather. In West Virginia, their walk to the one room schoolhouse had never been cancelled, no matter how deep the snow.

By noon the sun had come out and droplets of water were beginning to fall from the tree branches and wires. Everything had been so beautiful that they hated to see it start to melt. June and Cecil debated whether they should build a snowman or go into the woods and gather holly for Christmas decorations. The lure of the woods won. Bundling up in their warmest clothes, they set off across the road and disappeared among the trees.

Trying to remember where they had seen the holly, they walked farther than they had before. "Look over there!" June exclaimed. "I've never seen that before."

Following her gaze, he saw a tall stately house nestled among a stand of pine trees. "Do you think anyone lives there?" Cecil said. "If so, maybe they can show us where to find some holly."

They were hoping the house would be occupied, and that there would be someone at home. Right about now, a nice warm fire would feel pretty good. As they drew nearer, it was obvious the house had been abandoned. Some of the windows had been broken, and the shutters were hanging from the hinges.

Quickening his pace, Cecil said, "Let's see if we can get in." Her imagination going full speed, June hurried after him. "Why would anyone abandon a nice house like this?" she wondered. "Would it be safe to go inside?" Although she was too old to believe it might be haunted, from its looks she thought it could house a pretty fancy ghost.

As Cecil tried the door, it creaked open, causing them both to jump back a step. "Expecting a ghost?" June asked, laughingly. Cecil laughed, too, but for a second he looked like he'd rather be somewhere else.

They stepped across the threshold into a large entrance hall that led to a wide-open stairway with intricately carved woodwork. "I can picture Scarlet O'Hara coming down those steps in a beautiful hoop skirt," June said. "Doesn't it make you think of Gone With The Wind?"

Grinning devilishly he said, "It reminds me more of Boris Karloff or Dracula! Maybe if we look in the basement we'll find a vampire sleeping in his coffin."

"If you're trying to scare me, it's not going to work," she replied. "It's just an abandoned house. The only thing that could hurt us here is if the floor is rotten and we fell through it."

"It seems pretty sturdy. Let's look around," he said. Matching action to his words, he started moving from room to room. "Actually this place is in pretty good shape. I'm surprised no one is living here. As hard as it is to find a place to rent, I can't believe it's sitting here empty."

Standing by the kitchen window, looking into the overgrown backyard, June exclaimed, "Look what I found!" As Cecil came up beside her, she pointed to a large bush full of shiny green foliage and bright red berries. "We've found some holly. We'd better go get some and head for home."

Their arms full of holly, they followed their footprints back to more familiar territory. Before the house had disappeared from view, June looked back and again wondered about the people who had lived there. What had happened to cause them to abandon that nice house? Polly would say she was daydreaming again, but she knew there had to be a story behind it.

She asked Cecil, "What do you think happened to the people who lived here?"

He replied, "They moved out."

June retorted, "There has to be more to it than that."

"Like what?" Cecil asked.

June dramatically replied, "Maybe the owner was an author who wrote a popular novel. He went to Hollywood to write the screenplay for his book where he fell in love with an actress and stayed in Hollywood with her."

"Gee, June, you have quite an imagination." Secretly he enjoyed her stories, but didn't tell her.

As they walked toward the farmhouse, they glimpsed Mrs. Morrison and Meredith through the front window. June ran to the door, and when Meredith's mother opened it she asked, "Mrs. Morrison do you know why the house in the woods is deserted?"

She supplied the answer, "The man who lived there went away to the war in Europe in 1914 and never returned."

Inquisitive June asked, "What happened to him?"

Mrs. Morrison responded with, "No one knows."

Disappointed with the answer but still intrigued by the mystery, June took a deep breath and sighed.

Then hearing the tea kettle whistle, Mrs. Morrison rushed into the kitchen. After she left the room, Cecil surprised Meredith and June when he exclaimed, "I bet June can tell you what happened."

Meredith, who was familiar with June's flights of fancy, smiled waiting for June's explanation.

Taking the challenge, June thought for a few seconds before she launched into the story she had just concocted, "The handsome young soldier was injured in France, but he didn't die as most people think. He was discovered by a young French girl who nursed him back to health."

"After they fell in love and got married, he stayed in France. He was an excellent woodcarver, as we could tell from the looks of the staircase in the house in the woods. Then with his wood-crafting and carpenter skills, he helped her and her neighbors rebuild their small village."

Meredith and Cecil smiled and nodded before Meredith pronounced, "Sounds good to me!"

As the weeks went by, June and Cecil would return to the house in the woods where she would embellish the stories of the adventures of the young soldier who never returned. Cecil felt as though he was listening to a radio serial, and sometimes expected the soldier to come back to the house and join in the conversation. While they would have welcomed him, he never returned.

~

They had the trailer decorated for Christmas. The only thing missing were presents under the tree. "I'd like to go into Baltimore and do some shopping," Polly informed Burrel one evening as they were leafing through the Sears Roebuck catalogue. "We could order from here, but it would be fun for the kids to see the Christmas decorations in the city."

Burrel agreed, and they set off early the next Saturday, arriving in Baltimore by lunch time. They spent the day going from store to store. As Polly had predicted, June and Cecil loved everything about it; the tinsel and lights brightly decorating the stores, the Santa Claus on every corner, the sound of silver bells and the Christmas carols playing over the loud speaker in every store.

They sat at a lunch counter in Woolworths 5 & 10 Cent Store watching the smiles on some faces and the frowns on others as people went about the hustle and bustle of finishing their Christmas shopping. The excitement in the air had all four of the Harmans smiling. "I'm glad you thought of this, Mom," June said. "I've never seen anything quite like the way they celebrate Christmas in the city." She wasn't disappointed though to be returning to their Christmas in the country. While they'd been in Baltimore, they'd all done some secret shopping. As evidence, gaily wrapped Christmas packages were soon nestled under the tree.

Snow had softly fallen during Christmas Eve night, giving them the white Christmas they'd all wanted. They spent this, their first Christmas as a family together, at home. Even if they hadn't been too far away from their family or if they'd had the gasoline rationing stamps to make the trip, Burrel only had the one day off from work.

As Polly said grace, asking God "to bless all the loved ones we couldn't be with this Christmas," each person around the table was silent, thinking; Polly about her Mamma and Daddy, Burrel his Pap and his young son. June and Cecil's minds were on their mom and little brother.

Noticing the serious faces, Polly said, "This is a happy season. I cooked this turkey, and I expect everyone to eat heartily."

Cecil's response, "You don't have to ask me twice. Pass the mashed potatoes," brought laughter from all of them.

Merideth and June had exchanged small gifts. Merideth had gotten June a book, and June had given her a box of chocolate covered cherries. "I'm certainly glad, we don't still live at the Overbys," June thought. "This is a much better place to spend Christmas."

CHAPTER EIGHT
A MATTER OF JUSTICE

Meridith's parents were friendly neighbors. In fact, Polly soon found that Mr. Morrison was a little too much so. At first she felt uncomfortable around him, because of the way he looked at her. He made her feel he was undressing her with his eyes. "I'm probably just imagining it," she thought, "After all, he's old enough to be my father."

Even so, she thought she'd better mention it to Burrel. "I think that old man is a letch," she said. "Today he said you were a lucky man, having such a young wife. His wife was there when he said it, but it still made me feel uncomfortable."

Burrel didn't like the sound of it. "I'll just go over there and talk to him," he said. "You don't have to put up with that."

"The kids are happy here. Let's not do anything to jeopardize it. If he tries anything I'll just let him have it over the head with my iron skillet," she laughingly replied. "You know me. I won't put up with anything."

A few days later Polly was alone in the trailer when she heard someone at the door. Thinking it was Burrel returning from the store, she said, "You didn't take long," as she opened the door.

Standing on the bottom step was Mr. Morrison. "Burrel will be back in a minute," she said. "Did you want to see him about something?"

"No, I just came over to see you," he replied. "Aren't you going to ask me in for a cup of coffee?" Before she could reply, she felt something

77

on her leg. Looking down she saw his hand beginning to inch its way up her thigh.

Without taking a moment to think, she swung her foot forward catching him in the groin. Grabbing his crotch, he lost his balance and fell backwards into the snow. "Get out of here, you dirty old man, or you'll wish you had!" she stormed before slamming and securely locking the door.

He sat on the ground for a few seconds, then got up and dusting the snow from his trousers, limped off toward the farmhouse. She hadn't been watching him leave, so when she heard a sound at the door she thought it was him returning.

Grabbing her iron skillet, she threw open the door and shouted, "I thought I told you to get out of here!"

Her startled husband stared at her in shock and amazement. "What in the world is going on here?" he exclaimed.

"That letch! That dirty old man!" she said. "I went to the door thinking it was you, and Mr. Morrison was standing on the bottom step. While I was trying to get rid of him, he reached up and put his hand on my leg. I kicked him and knocked him off the step. I saw him land on the ground before I slammed the door."

"Are you alright?" he asked.

"I'm not only alright," she replied. "I'm great! I told you I could take care of it, and I did." From her tone and the glint in her eyes it was obvious that she was revved up on adrenalin. "Whether you know it or not, I learned a thing or two about taking care of myself when I was living alone," she proudly stated.

"I'm going over and have a little talk with that man. Right now!" Burrel proclaimed. Without another word, he was out the door and on his way to the farmhouse. She watched as he knocked, and Mr. Morrison opened the door and seemed to slither through it onto the porch. Burrel was stabbing his finger into Mr. Morrison's chest as he talked to him and Mr. Morrison was trying to back away. She couldn't hear what was said, nor did Burrel ever tell her, but the "letch" never caused her any more trouble.

~

A few days later while she was home alone she heard a car drive up alongside the trailer. As she looked out the window, she saw a tall, lanky sheriff's deputy walking toward the front door. Her first thought was something had happened to Burrel or to one of the kids.

Opening the door, her voice sounding frantic to her own ears, she demanded, "What is it? What's wrong?" His reassuring smile and the official looking document he was holding caused her to breath a sigh of relief.

"Nothing is wrong, Ma'am," the deputy responded. "If you're Mrs. Harman, I have a subpoena for you to testify as a witness in the trial of the Overbys. You are Mrs. Harman, aren't you?"

In response to her affirmative nod, he gave her the subpoena and a legal looking paper for her signature. While she was signing it, he remarked, "This county can use good citizens like you. We could get rid of some of this crime if more people were willing to testify." Touching his hand to the brim of his hat and saying, "Nice meeting you, Ma'am," he got into his cruiser and drove away.

Polly sat on the couch for a long time, first reading every word of the subpoena, then thinking about that horrible day when she and June had witnessed the brutal beating of the young man. Had the deputy inferred there would be danger in her testifying? She wasn't concerned about herself, but what about the kids?

She put the subpoena in her dresser drawer and busied herself preparing dinner. "I don't really think there is any reason to be afraid," she thought. "The only place June and Cecil go without me is in the woods. I can watch from here and see if anyone is hanging around. The Overbys have known all along that I plan to be a witness, and we haven't heard a word from them. I don't think we will now."

By the time June, Cecil, and Burrel arrived home, her fear was gone, and she was looking forward to her day in court. June's reaction to the news made her feel especially good. She was glad to hear her mom would be going into court and hoped all of these men would be sent to prison.

When she'd had time to think, unemotionally, about it, she had gotten over her first disappointment that her mom hadn't tried to stop the beating. She had come to the realization that if she had tried, those men would have seriously injured her, maybe even killed her. She couldn't imagine life without this woman. Deserving or not, Polly was once again, in June's mind, firmly ensconced on her pedestal.

With June's faith in her as an incentive, Polly bravely marched into the courtroom and staring into the eyes of the Overby father and sons, testified to what she had seen that day. After giving her testimony, she was allowed to stay and listen to the other witnesses. Their testimony proved to be as damning as hers had been. Polly and the other witnesses, her former neighbors, exchanged glances as the jurors, who had been out for less than an hour, filed back into the room. Their expressions were unreadable as the judge asked if they had reached a verdict.

"Yes we have," replied the white haired foreman. Following the judge's instructions to give the verdict to the bailiff, he handed him a white slip of paper and stood waiting while the judge silently read it.

Polly could see the tension on the defendants' faces and beads of sweat breaking out on the senior Mr. Overby's brow, as they watched this drama unfold. She couldn't help but enjoy watching them sweat, especially after seeing the victim and hearing that he might never recover from the head injuries he'd suffered.

Her thoughts were interrupted by the sound of the foreman reading the verdict. "We find the defendants guilty of all charges." With the words echoing in her ears, she stood up and quietly filed out of the courtroom with the rest of the spectators.

Standing, talking with the other witnesses outside the courthouse, they were joined by the young trooper they had met that violent day when this all began. "We did it," he said. "I told you we just needed some brave people to stand up to them, and you did. Unfortunately, we can't do anything about that poor young man, but by putting them away, we can keep it from happening to someone else."

"I just wish we could have stopped it," one of Polly's former neighbors said. Others in the group repeated her sentiments before they disbursed and headed their separate ways. They knew they couldn't go back and change that horrible day, but their actions today had helped make up for their lack of response during the attack.

Polly's report of the courtroom happenings held her family enthralled that evening. June was sorry she hadn't been able to be there, but especially she wished she had been old enough to testify. She'd have liked to add her voice to those who helped convict them. She sighed as she thought that even though she had passed her thirteenth birthday a month ago in January, in the eyes of the law she was still a child. Not for the first time, she thought, "I can't wait to grow up!"

CHAPTER NINE

A SNOW DAY

It was hard to believe that it had been a little over a year since they had first come together as a family. So much had happened in that time, not the least being all the places they had lived, and the people they had met.

Getting on the bus the Saturday they had to go to school to make up for the snow day they had missed, she saw Joy and Nadia's smiling faces greet her, and Ramon's turquoise eyes light up as she headed down the aisle to the seat he was saving for her. Sitting beside him with her friends across the aisle, she thought about how happy she was here and hoped they would be able to stay for a while.

This was one Saturday Burrel didn't have to work overtime. With June and Cecil in school, the house was quiet and he'd slept late. When he awoke Polly was sitting by the table sipping coffee and finishing a letter to her parents.

Seeing him sit up and stretch she said, "Good morning sleepy head. Are you about ready to get out of bed?" While he was crawling from under the covers and slipping on his trousers, she poured a steaming cup of coffee and sat it at his place at the table.

"I could use a few more mornings like this," he murmured. "These seven day work weeks are getting to me. As I remember, the good Lord himself worked six days, then had a day of rest."

While he was talking she stood up and fastened an organdy apron over her long sleeved flannel nightgown and turned toward the refrigerator for the bacon and eggs. "How about some scrambled eggs?" she asked.

"Okay, Granny," he said. "That sounds good to me."

"Who are you calling Granny?" she retorted saucily.

"Pulling her onto his lap and tousling her hair, he replied, "That thing you're wearing would make Betty Grable look like a grandma!"

Jumping up and flouncing across the room, she mimicked his words, "So this thing would make Betty Grable look like a grandma?" Then in her haughtiest voice she continued, "Is it the gown you dislike or the apron?"

"Oh, come on now. I can hardly see you at all in that flannel gown. The collar comes up to your chin and the sleeves look like they were made for a gorilla." He was smiling and enjoying their good-natured bickering. He liked to tease her, and he knew she enjoyed it and could certainly hold her own in any contest.

While he sat watching, she said, "You don't like it, uh? I certainly wouldn't want you to look at something you didn't like!" Then slowly and deliberately she reached behind her back and untied the sheer organdy apron, carefully folded it and draped it over the chair. Then unbuttoning the gown at the neckline, she stooped down, grabbed the hem, and in one fell swoop pulled it over her head and threw it in his face.

While he was sputtering and disentangling himself, she picked up the apron and again tied it around her waist. Then wearing only a smile and the sheer apron, she asked in her most sedate voice, "Now, how did you want your eggs?"

Reaching up and again pulling her onto his lap, he murmured, "It's not eggs I want now!" Much later, he said, "It's a good thing I didn't have to work today. I don't think I'd have made it on time." She only smiled, and looking at her watch said she knew he was right.

～

The next few days brought more snow, adding to the six inches already on the ground. When Cecil let their dog, Rex, outside, his white coat almost completely blended with his surroundings. "If he didn't have that patch of black around his eye, I don't know whether I could see him at all," he said.

The dog had developed a bad habit that made it necessary for them to keep an eye on him. He liked to chase Mr. Morrison's and the neighboring farmer's chickens, but worse yet they had caught him sucking eggs. Living in the country the way they did, this could be a serious problem and one hard to control.

The entire family had grown to love him since the day Burrel had brought him home as a tiny puppy when they'd lived at the Bush River Inn. When he had handed him to Cecil, this tiny white mongrel had looked around, squirmed out of Cecil's arms, jumped to the floor, and strutted around as if he owned the place. "He looks like he thinks he's king of the castle," Polly had exclaimed.

"King! That's what we'll call him," Cecil had said. "He looks like a king."

Watching him sniff his way around their tiny home, June had said, "With that black patch around his eye, he looks more like a pirate." Knowing he was the subject of their attention, he had walked over to where Cecil was sitting, and tried to jump up on his lap, but his puppy legs were still too short for him to make it. That didn't keep him from trying though.

Watching him, June and Cecil had engaged in some good-natured debating about his name. Cecil still wanted to call him King, and June was trying to come up with pirate names. "Blackbeard? Jolly Roger?" she mused. "No," she thought. "Neither one seemed to suit him."

Polly had started preparations for dinner, and was listening to their conversation. It didn't sound as though they were going to change their own or each other's minds. Deciding it might be a good idea if she intervened, she had asked June, "What do you have against calling him King?"

"I don't know. It just sounds so ordinary. I'd like him to have a special name," she had replied. Cecil had made a face at her response. It was clear he didn't think her suggestions were any better than his.

"I took Latin in high school," Polly said. "The word for king, in Latin, is Rex. What do you think of that for a name?" The puppy barked and wagged his tail, causing all of them to laugh. "Sounds to me as if he likes it. What do you think?" she had added. They had all agreed, and from then on he was Rex, their little king.

This problem with the chickens had started when they had first moved next door to the farmhouse. He was such a good companion for June and Cecil, and company for Polly when they were all away from home. He had become a big part of their family, and they couldn't imagine losing him. Determined to keep him close by and away from temptation, they kept a careful eye on him whenever he left the trailer.

CHAPTER TEN

ON THE ROAD AGAIN

A chance remark Polly made to Burrel a few days later solved their problem in a way none of them had ever imagined. They had gone into town grocery shopping, while June and Cecil were home working on their schoolwork. As Burrel drove toward Leonardtown, she pointed in the opposite direction and said, "I bet if we went that way, we'd end up in Mississippi."

"Mississippi?" he repeated. "You've never said anything before about going to Mississippi. Are you getting homesick?" he asked. She was pensive for a few seconds before replying, "I guess I am a little homesick. This is the longest I've ever been away from Mamma and Daddy. All this snow and cold weather is getting to me too. In Mamma's last letter she said the tulips are already blooming there."

"I know. You read that to me. I can't imagine tulips blooming in March," he said, as he drove over the snow-covered road. Earlier she had told him that if they hadn't met when they did she probably wouldn't have spent another winter up North.

"If I could, I'd turn this car around and head south," he said. "But I couldn't do that without a job. Besides the kids are still in school."

"If we went, you could find something. The depression is over. You haven't had any problem getting a job since the war started, have you? I think you could go if you wanted to," she said.

Glancing at her sitting beside him all bundled up in her camel's hair coat, wool scarf, gloves, and fur lined boots; he thought she looked like a little girl asking for a doll for Christmas. He reflected on all the things she had done for him and the children, and this was the first time she'd asked for anything this important. It would be hard to turn down this request.

With all his overtime they'd been able to save a thousand dollars. Since this was the first time they'd ever had that much money in the bank, he was feeling pretty good about it. He'd even managed to put a down payment on a fur coat for her. If they were ever going to be in a position to take a chance, it was now. Smiling at her he said, "Okay, Honey, let's go!"

When they got home they broke the news to June and Cecil that they were moving to Mississippi. Engrossed in their homework, it took a few seconds for them to comprehend what they had been told. "When are we going?" Cecil asked.

To Polly's response of, "Right away," June moaned, "But Mom, we can't leave now. I'm supposed to go to Ramon's house Friday to listen to his records." This was something they'd been talking about for months, and now, finally, Polly and his mother had worked out the details. She was going home with him on the bus, and Polly was going to pick her up after dinner.

Cecil, not any happier about the prospect than his sister, stated, "School won't be out for a couple more months. Couldn't we wait until then?"

"If we're going, it needs to be now. Your mom misses her mom and dad. She's spent all these months doing for us. It's about time we did something for her. Besides, you've never been in the south. I'm sure you'll like it. For one thing, it's already warm down there, warm enough for the flowers to already be in bloom." He had made some good points. They didn't want to be selfish by keeping Polly away from her family. The South in June's imagination was a beautiful place full of large white houses with tall stately columns gracing their front porches, their lawns dotted with magnolia trees. The South she pictured had all the glamour of Gone With The Wind. She weighed the desire to see this different part of the country against leaving her school and friends, but the decision wasn't going to be hers.

Looking into her parents' eager faces, she knew that no matter what she said, they were going. She also knew it would be hard for her to say goodbye to this place and these people. To protect herself from yet another separation, she built an even stronger protective armor around herself. It would be years before she again allowed herself the luxury of friends, and even then she only permitted a few to become close to her.

The last time she saw Joy, Nadia and Ramon they all promised to write, and Ramon vowed they'd see each other again even if they had to wait until they were grownup. Though she acted as if she believed him she could hear a cynical little voice in her mind saying, "Oh, sure. It seems to me I've heard that before."

Getting off the school bus, that last time, she didn't look back. She knew if she did, she'd cry, and that wasn't the picture she wanted to leave with her friends. She had already turned her back on them and her thoughts to her family's new adventure.

Leaving the next morning was reminiscent of their departure, a year before from Zanesville. The roads were covered with snow and more was falling. Unlike the other time, this car was snug and comfortable with a heater that was keeping the occupants warm. June, Cecil, and Rex were comfortable in the back seat, while Polly, studying a road map, sat next to Burrel in the front.

They were all approaching this trip as an adventure. Once they got underway they felt relaxed and excited. Polly, looking at the map, pointed out the states they would be traveling through, Virginia, North Carolina, Georgia, Tennessee and finally Mississippi.

"If we make good time, we should be almost to North Carolina tonight," Burrel said. But this was not to be. Instead, that night found them sleeping in a strange trailer in Baltimore. Unaware of what was about to happen, they were talking and peering out the windows at the passing scenery when, without the slightest warning, something slammed into them with a terrible force. They felt a tremendous jolt and simultaneously heard a grating, tearing sound. The car was pulled violently from one side of the road to the other.

Holding onto the steering wheel, Burrel fought to maintain control of the car and the wildly swaying trailer. While this battle was going on, an army truck whizzed by and skidded to a stop a short distance in front of them.

Burrel managed to bring the car and trailer to a stop behind it. While they sat in stunned disbelief, the young driver, a soldier, stumbled out, laughing hysterically. They clambered out of their car and looked back at the gaping hole in what had been their home. More than half of the wall on the left side of the trailer was gone.

The clothes that had been hanging in the closet were flapping loosely from the closet rod. Some had fallen onto the highway. Doors had been torn from the cabinets and dishes were smashed on the floor.

As they stared in horror at the shambles made of their home and their possessions, the soldier continued to laugh, an almost maniacal sound piercing the stillness of the countryside.

"How dare you laugh?" Polly screamed. "This is our home! You've wrecked our home!" Before anyone could stop her she had torn into him with her fists flying. "Stop laughing! Stop laughing! You are a mean, horrible person!" she sobbed.

Burrel and Cecil grabbed hold of her arms and pulled her away from him. "Polly, Polly," Burrel said in as calm a voice as he could manage. "He's not laughing. He's having hysterics."

In a matter of seconds a jeep with an army sergeant at the wheel and a corporal in the passenger seat pulled to a stop beside them. Taking in the scene of almost utter destruction, they were reminded of newsreels they'd seen of homes damaged by a tornado. Noticing the soldier sitting dejectedly in his truck, its entire right side scraped, told them what had happened. The sergeant assessed the situation as he walked over to Burrel, who was standing with his arms consolingly around an angry looking Polly. Next to them June stood with Cecil, who was holding a frantically barking Rex.

While the sergeant was talking to them, the corporal walked over to check out the young soldier's condition. While he didn't seem to be injured, he didn't appear to be in any condition to be of help to them.

Taking charge, the sergeant introduced himself as Sergeant Johnson and, after learning their names, asked Burrel if the car could be driven. Hearing it could be, he said, "We've set up camp a few miles back, for maneuvers. Pointing north, he added, "If you'll follow me I'll take you to our commanding officer, and we'll see what we can do about this situation."

Turning his attention to the young driver, he said, "You come along too. The C. O. will want to talk to you." After studying him more closely, and noticing his trembling hands, he continued, "I don't want you driving. Get in here with me, and the corporal will take your truck back to camp."

With the car and trailer sandwiched between the two military vehicles, the little caravan wound its way over the makeshift roads leading to the temporary army camp. Then getting out of the car, they trooped behind the sergeant over the snow and ice covered ground to one of the tents. Following his instructions to wait outside, they stood huddled together as if to protect themselves from the bitter cold while he disappeared through the front tent flaps.

When they were finally ushered in and introduced to the captain and his adjutant, they could still feel the cold creeping through their boots, chilling their toes. The kerosene stove gave out some heat, and the captain saw to it they were seated close to it while he asked questions of them and the young driver.

While the adjutant was filling out the necessary accident report, the sergeant saw to it the gaping hole in the side of the trailer was covered with a canvas tarpaulin. Before sending them on their way, the captain informed them the government would reimburse them for repair or replacement of the trailer.

He apparently believed what he was saying and probably never knew that it would be years before they would see any remuneration, and then only pennies on the dollar. The act of that young inexperienced soldier, driving on a snow covered road, was to wipe out the financial security Burrel and Polly had worked so hard to achieve. Instead of having a bank account to tide them over, while Burrel looked for a job, they had to use their savings to replace the trailer.

∼

After leaving the army camp, they had driven back to Baltimore to a mobile home dealership to see if the damage could be repaired. Their spirits soared when the dealer exclaimed, "I have seldom seen one I couldn't repair," only to plunge again when he continued, "but this is a first. There's no way to patch a hole that size. You're welcome to look around, but you won't find anyone else who can do it either."

Not ready to accept his judgment, they checked out a few other dealers only to hear the first one's words repeated. Sighing dejectedly, Burrel said, "I guess we don't have any choice, we're going to have to replace it."

They shopped around, settling on a bright blue one, its interior similar to the one they had lived in so briefly. By the time this transaction was completed, it was getting dark. "The dealer said we could park here for the night. I think we'd better take him up on it, don't you?" Burrel asked Polly.

Tired from the emotional strain and the physical aspect of moving their belongings from their damaged trailer, she quickly agreed. "If we go to bed now, maybe we can get an early start. One good thing," she said, "the snow has stopped and the wind has quit blowing. I don't think it's quite as cold here."

Sometime before daybreak Rex woke them with his barking. "Someone take that dog out!" Burrel muttered. "We've got to get some sleep if we're going to make that trip tomorrow."

Crawling out of bed, Cecil pulled on his coat and trousers, grabbed the leash, snapped it onto Rex's collar, and headed for the door.

Happy to be outside, Rex balked when Cecil tried to take him back inside. Looking out the door to see what was taking him so long and noticing that the sun was already beginning to come up, Polly told Cecil, "We'll be getting up shortly. Why don't you just tie him to the bumper and let him stay out for a while. He's going to be cooped up in the car long enough."

After Cecil fastened the leash securely to the car bumper, Rex happily pranced from side to side as far as it would reach. It was almost as though he knew he was going to be spending the next few days confined to the back seat of the car.

When, a little over an hour later, Cecil went outside to bring Rex in, he was gone. The leash was where he had tied it, but there was no sign of Rex. "Here Rex! Here Rex! Come on, Boy!" Cecil called.

Hearing him, June, Burrel, and Polly poked their heads out the door. "What's going on?" Polly asked. "Why did you unfasten Rex? He doesn't know his way around here. He could get lost!"

"I didn't unfasten him. He must have gotten out of his leash. It's still here, but he's gone!" Cecil was beginning to sound frantic as he continued to call and whistle for Rex.

By now they had joined him. While the rest of the family scoured the park and fanned out into the surrounding neighborhood, Burrel stooped down and examined the dangling leash. It didn't take long for him to discover that Rex hadn't gotten out of the leash alone. It had been cut. Seeing the cleanly severed fibers, he knew their search was useless.

By now, Rex would either be in one of the nearby houses or had been taken far away. This was something they were never to know. They had no choice but to give up the search, and continue on their trip, but until they were well out of Baltimore, they didn't give up hope of seeing him running, barking and wagging his tail, as if to say, "You can't leave without me." Looking out the rear view window, June silently mouthed, "Goodbye, little king." To help ease the pain, she pictured Rex in one of the many white stepped houses they'd passed, and had managed to convince herself that the person who'd taken him, most certainly, would give him a loving home.

～

Sad as they all felt, this was an adventure, one they started enjoying in spite of their loss. As the wheels turned, and the miles slipped away, it was like flipping the pages of the calendar forward. They could see the snowstorm give way to clear skies and only patches of snow remaining on the ground.

As they continued their journey, each day brought changing scenery. First the trees in bud, then their branches full of new leaves and the brown grass turned to green.

The fourth day of their trip brought them to the south June had read about. They passed white stately houses, with their columned verandas surrounded by wisteria, magnolia and azaleas in full bloom. In the woods, on the side of the road, they could see flashes of white, pink and red from the blossoms of the dogwood and redbud trees. With the warm sun and gentle breeze caressing their cheeks, it was hard to realize they had been wearing heavy coats, boots and gloves only four days earlier. They felt as if they had traveled a couple months forward in time.

"I can't believe we're almost there," Burrel said. "I'm not sure I could have gotten us another ration stamp." He was referring to the problems they'd had with flat tires and his dealings with the rationing board.

It seemed they'd had a tire blow out every couple hundred miles. Every time it happened, he'd had to pull over to the side of the road, replace it with the spare and start looking for the nearest office of the ration board. Before he could buy another tire he had to be issued a ration stamp.

"I'm so happy about almost being home, I don't know if I could summon up any more tears," Polly said. She was referring to one of the officials who had, at first, refused to issue Burrel a stamp, saying sarcastically, "Didn't you folks know there was a war on when you started on a trip like this? We can't be giving every Damn Yankee, who decides to escape from the snow, extra ration stamps. You've already used your quota and then some."

It had been obvious from the official's stern expression that Burrel was getting nowhere as he explained that since the trailer was brand new and the car only a few months old, he hadn't anticipated any problem with the tires. "When we started having trouble with flat tires, all we could get were recaps and they just haven't held up," he said. His further account of his months of driving to work at the various defense construction sites, and the resulting wear and tear on his tires hadn't changed the official's mind.

Grumbling about all the red tape he'd had to face on this trip, he'd gotten back into the car. "That is the most bull-headed man I've ever encountered," he said. "I can't talk him into letting us have another stamp, no matter what I say! If he doesn't change his mind, we're going to be stranded here, or we can go on without a spare and just hope we can make it to Mississippi."

"Let me give it a try," Polly said. "I'll bet I can get that stamp." Burrel couldn't imagine how she could, if he couldn't, but he could no more have stopped her than he could have stopped the river from flowing.

Applying a fresh coat of lipstick and running a comb through her long red hair, she left Burrel and Cecil waiting in the car while she and June marched up the steps and disappeared through the same door Burrel had so recently exited.

In about forty-five minutes it opened, and they could see Polly and June standing in the hall, smiling and talking to the official as if they were old friends. Seconds later when they emerged, Polly was waving a sheet of white paper. "I got it!" she said as Burrel reached across and opened the door for her.

Scooting across the seat to sit beside him she drawled, "First I managed to squeeze out a couple tears like I did the last place, but I wouldn't have needed to. Once I opened my mouth, and he could tell I wasn't a Yankee, I didn't have a bit of trouble. I just explained it was too cold up North and I couldn't stand all the snow any longer, and how I just had to come back home to be with my Mamma and Daddy."

Laughing, Burrel said, "If we have any more flats, I'm not going to waste any more of my time. I'll just send you into the ration board office in the first place."

"What do they mean calling us Yankees?" June asked. In newsreels, she'd heard our troops overseas called Yankees, but announcers using the name had sounded respectful, even admiring, not in the belittling way this man had been toward her dad.

"Don't be so serious about it," Polly said. "That's just a term people down here use when they talk about anyone from north of the Mason Dixon line. It's not just Yankee, it's Damn Yankee, as if it's one word."

"Polly," Burrel exclaimed, disapprovingly. "Watch your language!" They didn't use profanity in their house, and he was surprised to hear it coming from her mouth.

She laughed, "That's not cuss words down here. That's part of our language, but no one means anything by it." This trip was the first time any of them had heard the term, but certainly was not to be the last.

CHAPTER ELEVEN

AN UNFRIENDLY PLACE

Fortunately, they completed their journey without the telltale sound of another tire blow out. By evening they found themselves driving up the lane to Polly's girlhood home. A tall baldheaded man came out on the porch to greet them. "Daddy!" Polly called, as she jumped out of the car and ran toward him.

As they hugged, and the tall man in his soft southern voice said, "How's my Wampus Cat?" June, Cecil, and Burrel stood by the car, silently watching. Finally turning her attention to them, Polly said, "Come on up here. I want you to meet my Daddy."

Striding forward, Burrel extended his hand to his new father-in-law, and said, "I'm glad to meet you, Sir." While the two men were sizing each other up, they were interrupted by Polly bringing her suddenly shy teen-agers forward to meet their new grandfather. Bathed in the warmth of his warm friendly smile, they felt welcome and knew instantly they were going to like this man.

They had to wait until the next day to meet Polly's mother. While Polly's father lived on the farm and worked as a telegraph operator at the railroad station in Brandon, her mother lived in Jackson in an apartment building owned by Polly's Aunt Carol. She usually came home on the weekends. Ten years older than her husband, she no longer felt her health was good enough to withstand the rigors of farm living.

She had two grandchildren, David's daughter, Barbara Jean, and Ruby's son, Marion. Since they both called her Nanny, Polly told

June and Cecil they were to do the same. This new Nanny, the first grandmother June was to know, was a tiny woman, the red in her hair darkened, but still evident.

Polly had told them her Mamma had been raised to be a helpless woman. That she often appeared to be overwhelmed by life, not the least being her life on the farm or the antics of her younger daughter.

She had despaired when Polly had left nursing school in New Orleans and taken off on her own to live "up North". Although she would come to care for her new step-grandchildren, she hadn't been at all pleased when she heard her daughter had wed a divorced man with three children, and that she would be raising two of them. She also felt Polly had married beneath herself.

Of course, she had felt the same about her own marriage to Polly's father, but they had been happy together. Growing up privileged, she had been pampered by her attorney father and socially active mother. As a young woman, her best friends had been the governor's daughters. Before her first marriage she had gone to many parties and dances in the governor's mansion.

Her life with Will Srite had been happy though it was different from her life in her father's home, or with her first husband, the minister. Having been raised to believe that it was a woman's duty to marry, bear and raise children, she was satisfied that she had done her duty.

She had borne four; David, Ruby, Fred, and Polly and raised five, her four and Will's son Cecil. Now that phase of her life was over, she felt she had earned the right to live her life in a more genteel manner. If living in town made "Miss Maggie" happy, it was all right with her husband, "Mr. Will".

This title of respect shown to adults was new to June and Cecil. Polly had instructed them to call the adults, in the family's circle of friends and neighbors, by their first names preceded by Miss for the females and Mister for the males. This was true, regardless of their marital status.

They had done this in West Virginia with their school teachers, Miss Lily and Miss Nina, and in Maryland with Miss Phoebe and Miss Jane, but the teachers were the exception to this rule, though, in their new school. They were to be called by their last names preceded by the appropriate title.

∼

By the end of the week, the family had settled into a park in Jackson, June and Cecil had started to school, and Burrel began job hunting. Neither experience turned out to be successful or happy ones.

Burrel soon found there was no defense building going on in or near Jackson, and that local builders had all the help they could use. For the first time in years he was unable to find a job. He was beginning to feel their hasty decision to come here had been a mistake, especially now that their savings had been wiped out by the trailer disaster.

His mortification was complete, when Polly had to ask her father for a loan. Always able to provide for her, until now, he was humiliated. "What kind of man does her father think she has married?" he asked himself. "Tell him," he told Polly, "I will find a job even if it means we have to go back to Maryland."

"Daddy will understand," she said. "We're not the first family members he's helped. I remember, during the depression we'd have one family after the other coming to the farm to live. Daddy always said that as long as he had a job and they didn't, and as long as we had food to put on the table, they were welcome."

"I know, but that was during the depression. A lot of people were out of work then. These are supposed to be better times," he said. It was becoming abundantly clear to him, he was going to have to do something...and do it soon.

Polly's brother Fred had heard of their dilemma and called from Baton Rouge, Louisiana to tell them about a construction project starting there. Working through the union, Burrel was able to get a job. Leaving June and Cecil with Nanny, Polly went with him to help him find a place to live.

This accomplished, she was ready to return to Jackson, but after his first day on the job he returned from work with a raging fever. Immediately getting him to bed and piling covers over him, she started him on aspirin and fluids and put in a call to the doctor.

After examining Burrel, he was puzzled by this illness, finally diagnosing it as a fever of unknown origins. Burrel was very ill, and the doctor was concerned for his recovery. In his opinion, he needed to be in the hospital with around the clock nursing care. When Polly explained that she was a nurse, and told him of their financial difficulties, he relented and let him stay at home.

The landlady was unhappy with this arrangement, though. Openly hostile to her, she acted as if Polly had invented Burrel's illness to be able to stay in the room. Stomping up the steps, she could be heard muttering that she had rented the room to one man, and now "that woman", as she called Polly, was staying with him. Not only that, but she was turning the boarding house into a hospital.

After a week of Polly and the doctor's good care, his fever finally broke. Still weak and unable to return to work, the doctor advised him to rest for at least another week. Concerned the fever might recur, Polly braved the landlady's wrath and stayed a few days longer.

～

While he was recuperating, Burrel contacted the electrician's union in Zanesville to check on availability of jobs. He'd had it here and was ready to return to Maryland if that was what it would take to again be able to support himself and his family.

The news was better than he had expected. Kaiser Aluminum Company was building a large factory about four or five miles outside Newark. "The job in Newark is a big one and will last for over a year. If I stay here I will be out of work in a couple months. Then, where will we be? I'm going to take that job at the aluminum plant. And that's all there is to it!" he firmly informed Polly.

She knew him well enough to know that when he spoke in that tone, there was no need to argue. Usually good natured, he had reached his limit of tolerance, and once he'd gotten to that point there was no way he was going to change his mind. She didn't have to be reminded that too many things had happened to him since they'd arrived here, and she couldn't blame him for looking on the South as an unfriendly place.

She also knew how much not being able to take care of his family had bothered him and how humiliated he'd been when he'd had to go to his new in-laws for money. If that hadn't been bad enough, he'd almost died from this unknown fever.

As if their thoughts were on the same wavelength, he grimly said, "This is one Damn Yankee who's going home!"

Even though she hated the prospect of having to leave her parents so soon, she knew he was right. The job market wasn't going to improve for him here. After a lengthy discussion they decided Polly, June, and Cecil would stay in Jackson until school was out. This would give her a chance to spend some time with her family. He would take the car and trailer to Ohio with him.

Polly made arrangements for them to stay with her mother while he was gone. When school was out they would travel by train to join him. This wasn't an ideal arrangement, but she consoled herself by thinking it would only be for a couple months.

∼

It seemed as if the South wasn't through with him yet. He'd only been on the road a few hours when he heard the sound of a siren behind him. "Wonder who they're after," he thought as he glanced in his rear view mirror and slowly eased his car to the right.

To Burrel's amazement, a sheriff cruiser stopped in front of him, and a beefy looking deputy got out and swaggered over to the car. "Where do you think you're going in such a hurry?" he asked.

Burrel couldn't believe his ears. He knew that when he was pulling the trailer, there was no way he could exceed the speed limit. "I was only going forty-five miles an hour," he explained.

"Oh, so you admit you were going forty five?" the trooper said. "This is a thirty-five mile an hour zone."

"How could it be?" Burrel asked. "I've been on this road for hours, and every sign I've seen has been for a fifty mile an hour speed limit."

The deputy's voice hardened as he continued, "You're in our county now, and we have a thirty-five mile an hour speed limit. You were exceeding it, and I'm going to have to take you in."

To Burrel's words of protest, the deputy snapped, "Don't give me any of that Damn Yankee lip. You'll have your chance to talk to the judge in a few minutes."

As Burrel followed the cruiser, he thought, "Surely the judge will listen to me. I really need to get going." This turned out to be wishful thinking on his part. Unfortunately, he had driven through a speed trap. The locals were aware of it, but many hapless travelers found themselves in Burrel's situation.

The judge's mind was as closed as the deputy's had been. Burrel soon found himself pronounced guilty, given the option of paying a hundred dollar fine or going to jail. With his one call he was able to contact Polly to see if she could get the money and wire it to him. During the hours he waited for the money to arrive from her father he suffered yet another humiliation. He was put in a cell with a couple drunks and a man in a business suit, who, looked up forlornly at Burrel and commented, "I bet you're a speed trap victim too."

Burrel replied, "I sure am! I thought I was driving under the speed limit."

"Our punishment is a fine, jail, and these fleas," the businessman lamented, as he vigorously scratched his legs.

Burrel responded with, "Oh, no! Can it get any worse?" Just then one of the drunks started coughing and spewed vomit on Burrel's shoes.

Burrel thought, "I guess that answers that question."

When the money arrived and he was released, he went to a pay phone and called Polly. She told him to return to Jackson at least for the night. It had only been a few days since he'd been so ill, and she was worried about him. Feeling queasy, and not knowing whether he was getting sick or suffering from the emotional strain, he once again turned toward Jackson and the comfort of his family.

He drove directly to the farm where Polly was spending the night. Before he even went inside he started peeling off his clothes and instructing her to burn them. "They're filthy from the jail, and they're full of fleas," he said. "I'd wear my good suit," he explained. "But someone stole it from the car when it was parked in the jail parking lot."

"I can't blame you for wanting to get out of here," Polly's dad said, "But believe me, the South isn't always so inhospitable to strangers. There are a lot of good people living here."

In meeting Will Srite, Burrel knew he had been fortunate in meeting one of those "good people". He didn't think they came any better. It was easy to understand why Polly was so close to him. Although Burrel was embarrassed at all that had happened, he was glad he'd had the chance to meet this kind man.

These thoughts were interrupted by Polly's dad's voice, "You just happened to be a victim of a kangaroo court. The judge and sheriff are working together on it. In their county they set up lower speed limit signs, but they're usually placed where they're not easily seen. Mostly, they catch people from out of state. The sheriff couldn't get reelected if he tried that trick on the locals."

Burrel said, "Believe me, I'll watch out for the lower speed limit signs when I get on the way again tomorrow." A good hot bath and a good night's sleep helped him, body and mind. The next day he again said goodbye to his family and headed north. He arrived in Ohio a few days later, this time without any unpleasant incidents.

CHAPTER TWELVE
DAMN YANKEES IN THE SOUTH

June and Cecil were trying to adjust to the differences here. They really enjoyed meeting the rest of Polly's family and the kindness and slow easy pace of the people they met. They also liked being able to go downtown where they'd go to the movies, walk along the street, and browse through the stores and listen to the sound of the soft southern voices.

Other things produced culture shock. Not the least being the contrast in the way black and white people were treated. June found it difficult to believe that black people weren't allowed to eat at lunch counters or restaurants with whites, or sit on the bus with them. She had started to sit in the back of the bus, only to be told, "Whites sit in the front and the nigras in the back."

When she went to the movies she became aware negroes were relegated to the top balcony. They weren't even allowed to use the same water fountain and were expected to step off the sidewalk if a white person walked by.

Yet the negroes who worked in the house or on Granddad Srite's farm were treated with respect. Polly said the woman working in the house, and the man in the fields, had worked for her family since she was a little girl. Calling them Aunt Lee and Uncle Dent, it was obvious she was very fond of them.

Aunt Lee and Uncle Dent's granddaughter, Maddie, lived with them. Since the two races weren't allowed by law to attend school together, and the school bus was provided for white students only, it was difficult for Maddie and other black children to get to school. June was dismayed at the injustices of these practices, especially when she got to know Maddie and discovered how interested she was in reading and learning about the world beyond the farm. June brought books home from the school library for Maddie to read and enthralled her with stories of her family's life in West Virginia and their vagabond years.

~

June attended Bailey Junior High School. It was one of the most beautiful schools she had ever seen, but within its walls she spent some very unhappy moments. The first day in class she met a freckle faced redheaded boy named Johnny Townsend. He greeted her by asking, "What side of the Civil War did your ancestors fight on?" In response to her blank expression, he said, "You must be a Damn Yankee."

Before the day was over, she'd heard the same question and been called the same name more than once. By the time she got home she was fuming. "What's this stuff about the Civil War?" she asked Polly. As far as she was concerned, the Civil War belonged in the history books.

Polly explained that to people here, the Civil War was still a sore spot. There were those still living whose parents or grandparents had lost everything during that war. June looked at her incredulously. This made no more sense to her than it had today in the cafeteria when the server had ladled gravy over her white rice. To her way of thinking, rice was to be eaten as a cereal with cream and sugar or in a pudding. "Gravy on rice!" she thought, "Yuk! Double yuk!"

For the first time in her life she hated going to school. Each day she wondered what new torture they were going to devise. When she was combing her hair in the rest room, between classes, a girl from her English class said, loudly enough to be sure everyone could hear, "That new girl sure does talk funny." In response another giggling girl had agreed, then added, "They sure do grow them tall up North."

During June's next class she felt the most excruciating pain she'd ever felt. It hit without warning, spreading from her forehead to behind her eyes and into her temples. The aspirin given to her by the teacher didn't help at all, so she was sent to the nurse's office. After finding that having her lie down with a cold compress on her forehead wasn't easing the pain, she issued a pass and told her to go home. While engulfed in waves of pain, June made her way to the bus stop, waited the ten minutes for it to arrive, rode it downtown, transferred and rode the second bus to within minutes of home.

Polly was alarmed at the sight of her daughter coming home at this time of day. After hearing about the pain she immediately had her go to bed, darkened the room by pulling the blinds, and called the doctor. Inadvertently, before he arrived, June discovered a treatment that was to work this time and when the pain recurred in the future.

Lying in the darkened room, crying from the pain, she eventually fell asleep. When she awoke, although she felt weak and drained, the pain was gone. This doctor said, as the one in Baton Rouge had said about Burrel, this too was of unknown origin.

That weekend, June and Cecil met Polly's brother Fred and his wife, "little" Polly. Being smaller, the family had started calling her that when both Pollys had the last name of Srite.

During the day the conversation turned to school. Though June had meant to keep her problems to herself, Uncle Fred and Granddad Srite were so kind and interested that she found herself telling them some of the things kids had said to her. She explained, "I'm afraid I'll never fit in because I'm so different."

"You know," Granddad Srite said, "I remember a time when I was probably about your age, maybe even a little younger. There was a boy in my class who always did everything better than any of the rest of us. I really wanted to be like that boy and would find myself imitating him."

"Well, one day in class the teacher said, just for fun, the next day we were going to have a contest to see who could make the funniest face. There would be first, second, and third place winners. I'm sure most of the kids went home and practiced making funny faces. Not me, though. I had decided I was going to watch this other boy and what ever kind of face he made, I was going to copy it."

"I figured he would win first prize, and I would come in second. I watched him closely and when it came my turn I made a face just like he had. Imagine my surprise when the names of the winners were called, and I wasn't one of them."

"After the prizes were awarded, the teacher asked me if I'd stay after class and help clean the blackboard. I soon found out, she had just used that as an excuse to talk to me alone. What she told me that day really made a difference to me."

"She said that I had made a very funny face, probably the second funniest, but she'd seen me watching the other boy and copying him. She told me, "If you want to win in my class, you have to be an original. You don't have to be like anyone else. You're a unique person. I would give you a lot more credit for being yourself, giving it your best try, than I would give a perfect copy. Remember, you are one of a kind. Don't try to be like anyone else."

"After I went home that evening I mulled over her words and found they made a lot of sense. I never forgot what she said, and I never tried to be like anyone else after that."

Looking at June's serious upturned face, he added, "You're just fine the way you are. You didn't grow up in the South, so you're not going to talk like we do, but you don't have to. The way you talk is just fine. Just remember what my teacher said, it's important to be you. Another thing, that girl who said what she did about you being tall probably envies you. I've found that a lot of times when someone says something to hurt someone else's feelings, it's because they're jealous. Remember, it's alright to be tall, and it's also fine to be short or in-between. We're all different, and that's the way it was meant to be."

Then smiling, he added, "Just think how confusing it would be if we all looked alike." This brought another smile to her face, as she looked around the room, picturing everyone wearing the same face.

When Granddad Srite quit talking, Uncle Fred had picked up on the conversation, his voice soft and slow, "The best way for you to handle that red-headed boy is to pretend that whatever he says doesn't bother you. It's no fun picking on anyone if they just ignore you. That redheaded boy will probably leave you alone if you can come up with the right response. I bet my sister can think of some that will shut his mouth."

When they returned to the apartment that night, they practiced some responses for June to use. She didn't have to wait long to find out whether or not they'd work. In study hall the next day when Johnny leaned over and said, "Hey, Yankee, I'll bet you have a blue belly," June tossed her head, sending her hair flying away from her face, stuck her nose in the air and haughtily replied, "That's something you'll never know."

Johnny didn't reply, but the red flush that crept from under his collar didn't stop until it had blended with his red hair. That was answer enough. This was fun, she could hardly wait for the next one.

It came when she placed her order in the cafeteria and a girl behind her in line remarked to another girl, "I see what you mean, that new girl does talk funny." Turning to face her, June smiled sweetly and said, "Why don't you come up North sometime. Everyone up there can tell you how funny you sound."

A few more responses like that and their remarks came to an end. In fact, when she no longer had to defend herself, she started to look around and listen. Much to her surprise she found this was a pretty interesting place after all, and as her dad always said, "There were things to learn."

A few days later she found herself smiling during assembly when all the students were singing a new patriotic song. Everyone except her was singing, "Let's Remembah Pearl Harbah" while she sang, "Let's Remember Pearl Harbor." "Granddad is right," she mused, as the girl sitting next to her turned and smiled. "Who cares if our accents are different? It's okay." Secretly, though, she thought, "In this case, everyone is singing it wrong, except me."

~

Polly had decided she wanted them to have a better impression of her home state. "Come on kids," she said. "Just because it will be a couple months until we can join your dad, doesn't mean we're going to sit around and mope. There are things to do, and places I want you to see."

That sounded good to June and Cecil. They were ready for some fun. Polly had a reason for mentioning it that particular afternoon. She'd been flipping through the pages of the paper and had seen that a movie, The Chocolate Soldier, starring Nelson Eddie was playing at a movie house somewhere across town.

"I don't know where it is, but we'll find it," she told them, as they stood waiting for the bus to arrive. The driver told them which transfers they'd need to make. If she'd known how far it was, or that it would be almost midnight before they got home, she might not have taken them on a school night.

Though they were bleary eyed the next morning, they were glad they'd gone. Despite the fact a singer named Rise Stevens, rather than his usual co-star, Jeanette McDonald, played opposite Nelson Eddie, they had enjoyed the outing.

It had seemed like an adventure, even to Polly, who had discovered an unfamiliar part of town. From the bus window they'd seen several beautiful white columned houses. This was the South June had dreamed about, one she'd caught glimpses of before. With her vivid imagination she could almost picture Scarlet O'Hara, with her arm linked through Rhett Butler's, flirtatiously looking up into his eyes as the two of them strolled across the veranda.

Saturdays found them browsing through the downtown stores, looking and listening more than shopping. Sales clerks commented on their accents, not in a disparaging way, but as if they were interested in them.

It didn't take long to discover that they weren't the only newcomers in this striving city. Everywhere they went they saw handsome young men in Army Air Corps uniforms, who were stationed at the nearby Air Corps base. From the sound of their accents it was obvious they were from all parts of the country from Brooklyn to California. Intermingling with these accents were airmen speaking a totally unfamiliar language.

Learning their story brought the war closer than it had ever been to June and Cecil. These men were Dutch and Javanese airmen serving with the United States Air Corps. When the Netherlands had been occupied by the Germans, the servicemen had managed to make their way to the United States. According to stories being circulated, many of them knew nothing of what might have happened to their families at home.

June could sympathize with them. She knew what it was like to be separated from people you loved. At least in her case, she knew where they were, and that they were safe. As she observed these young men, she prayed that when this war was over and they were able to go home, they would find their families safe. From conversations she'd overheard, she was afraid this wouldn't always be the case.

~

The next member of the family they were to meet was Polly's brother, their new uncle Cecil. He resembled his father and his brother Fred, including the receding hairline. Like his brother he was very handsome. Unlike Fred, who was an enlisted man, Cecil was an officer in the Army Corps of Engineers. He and his wife, Ella, a pretty dark haired young woman, were kind and friendly to their new niece and nephew.

When he was introduced to his new uncle, Cecil quipped, "It's groovy having an uncle with the same name. It makes us really sound related."

Shaking his new nephew's hand, he responded, "I already think we are."

Cecil was impressed with the thought of what life would be like as an officer and started behaving the way he thought one would act. After acting out his fantasies by barking orders to June, she put up with it for awhile, but finally shot back with, "Stop that! You're not the colonel! Uncle Cecil is!"

Polly heard them and interjected, "That's not Uncle Cecil's way. He wouldn't talk to anyone like that."

Chagrined, Cecil said, "I guess you're right, but it was fun while it lasted."

Completing the family picture was Polly's sister Ruby, a nurse, and her husband a buyer at a prestigious downtown department store. A slender redhead, ten years Polly's senior, she had sometimes acted more like a mother than older sister to her.

The sisters' feelings toward each other were ambiguous. While there was love between them, they each wanted to change the other. Polly wanted Ruby to be less demanding, to let her be herself, while Ruby wanted Polly to be less rambunctious, more of a lady, like she and their mother.

Neither would ever change the other. Polly was too earthy to ever fit her sister's definition of a lady, and Ruby enjoyed her genteel lifestyle. In Burrel, June, and Cecil's minds, though, Polly did possess the qualities of a real lady. She was a loving, caring person who had managed to bring some order into their chaotic existence.

Like her mother, Ruby was not pleased that her sister had married a man with a ready-made family. She was also dismayed that she had been living a vagabond life in such dismal spots. In a trailer, of all things!

She and Paul lived in a beautiful apartment, which he had exquisitely decorated. Every piece of furniture, glassware, silver or china, and every wall hanging had been chosen to reflect their cosmopolitan taste.

Neither woman would have been happy with the other's lifestyle. It was to be years before they learned to recognize or appreciate each other's admirable qualities. By then Ruby was to acknowledge that marrying Burrel and acquiring June and Cecil was the smartest thing Polly had ever done.

~

Ruby's first marriage had ended disastrously, leaving her as a single mother with a baby son. Without help from the boy's father, she'd found it difficult to raise a child alone. Her aunt, her mother's sister Carol (pronounced Carl) and her husband Simmie Gaston were childless. At first they had taken care of the baby, Marion, while Ruby worked. After awhile she had allowed them to adopt him. Although Marion lived with Aunt Carol and Uncle Simmie, Ruby managed to see him often. He was in the unique position of having two mothers.

Aunt Carol and Uncle Simmie were old enough to be his grandparents. Since they had waited so long to have a child they could deny him nothing, nor could Ruby. June was to find this out the hard way while she, Polly and Cecil were staying with Nanny.

The building that housed three apartments was constructed like a raised ranch. Aunt Carol, Uncle Simmie, and Marion lived in the front apartment, a middle-aged couple in the side one, and Nannie on the lower level.

Polly was fond of her aunt and uncle, whom she, June, and Cecil visited often. June and Cecil liked Polly's short, roly-poly uncle and his tall dignified wife. Most of all, June loved Marion's little Pekinese, Toy.

While the adults were visiting, she would sit on the couch, holding him on her lap, brushing his soft fur, and talking to him.

Marion had grown tired of the dog, and Aunt Carol decided to find a new home for Toy. Noticing how much June and Toy seemed to like each other, she asked June if she would like to have him. Still missing Rex, June jumped at the chance to have another dog, especially one as wonderful as this one.

It turned out that Toy was to be hers for a very short time. A couple days later when she returned from school, she ran into the apartment calling his name. Instead of his usual excited greeting, she was met by silence. Walking into the kitchen, she asked Polly, "Where's Toy? He didn't come when I called."

The flush of color on Polly's cheeks alerted her that something was wrong. This was a telltale sign that she was either upset or angry. To her repeated inquiry about Toy, Polly replied, "Aunt Carol came down and got him. She said it was upsetting to Marion having Toy in the same building. Seeing him every day, the way he would, he'd miss him too much."

"You mean Marion wanted him back?" June asked. Remembering how much they had all missed Rex, she could understand how Marion must have felt. He probably hadn't realized how much he was going to miss the little dog until he was gone. "At least I can still see Toy," she said.

"I'm afraid not," Polly replied. "Aunt Carol told me that Marion didn't want him back. He just didn't want him living so close where he'd be reminded. She gave him to someone else, someone who doesn't live in the building." As she uttered these last words, she looked as sad as June felt.

"She gave him to someone else?" June wailed. "How could she do that? She gave him to me!" Despite all efforts to console her, June was hurt, angry, and disappointed. She had really loved that little dog, and she was never to forget him.

Years later, when she had children of her own, a toy collie came into their lives. While most people thought he was named Toy because of his size, June and Polly remembered his namesake. He was probably the only collie ever to be named after the memory of a Pekinese.

~

June and Cecil were excited as the school year was coming to a close, and they were facing the prospect of seeing their father again. Looking out the classroom window, watching the military planes flying in formation, she reflected that this was a pretty nice place after all. Even Johnny Townsend, sitting across the row from her, no longer looked so hateful. Since he'd quit teasing her, he'd talked to her about wanting to be grown, so he could join the Army Air Corp and fly planes like the ones they'd become accustomed to seeing and hearing overhead. Remembering living outside Washington, wanting to hurry and grow up, so she could be a government girl, she understood how he felt.

The media glamorized the war and stirred people to a patriotic fervor. The news reports, the movies, and the songs people were singing made young people feel frustrated that they were too young to get involved in any way to bring this horrible war to an end. Although the children and teen-agers all helped the war effort by collecting tin cans and other scrap metal to be changed into materials to build fighting equipment, that wasn't the same as helping to fight.

~

Before embarking on their trip to Ohio they spent one last Saturday on the farm with Polly's dad and mother. June and Cecil had become fond of their new grandparents and felt a twinge of sadness at leaving them. Granddad Srite was full of wisdom he had spent his life imparting to his own children. Now, as the new grandchildren in the family, it was their turn.

When he told them he hoped they would take some southern customs "back up North", June was sure she would. Hadn't she already learned to say "hey" instead of "hi", and didn't she eat grits with her scrambled eggs?

Unfortunately, while she was nodding her agreement, she was passed the rice followed by a bowl of gravy. Since everyone was watching her, she thought, "Why not?" and ladled the thin brown liquid over the white grain.

Then feeling as much enthusiasm as she would have if her plate had been full of squiggly worms, she dipped her fork into it and raised a forkful to her mouth. Her look quickly changed from distaste to one of enjoyment. Why hadn't she tried it before? It was actually good.

Watching her, everyone laughed, except Granddad Srite, who nodding his approval, said, "Don't be afraid to try something new. Miss Maggie wouldn't put anything on the table that didn't taste good."

Listening to him, made her think of her own father and Grandpap and the many words of wisdom she'd heard from them. She was glad she would be seeing her dad soon and hoped it wouldn't be too long before they could visit her grandpap and the rest of the family in West Virginia.

Looking out the window on the last day of school, June's gaze again followed the flight of the military planes flying in perfect formation. Watching until they disappeared into the clouds, her thoughts wandered to the things she, Polly, and Cecil had done while they were living here, things she'd seen or heard, and the people she'd met.

She knew she would always remember the sheer beauty of the city, the kindness shown by Polly's family, the soft voices and accents of people they met. On the other hand, she hoped she'd soon forget the title "Damn Yankee" that had been bestowed upon her.

Although she and Cecil had found girls and boys their own age to spend some time with after school, they hadn't made close friends. This made it much easier to leave this place than any other. This was not the case with Polly. She was leaving her family and girlhood home, not knowing when she'd be able to return.

CHAPTER THIRTEEN
THE JOURNEY HOME

The long awaited day finally arrived, and the very air at the station was charged with emotion, running the gamut from happiness and anticipation to sadness and despair. Waiting for the arrival of their train, June, Polly, and Cecil sat on a bench, observing the drama unfolding around them. Men, women and children, who had been standing watching a train pull into the station, would suddenly run with outstretched arms to enfold a young serviceman as he stepped off the train. This would be followed by joyful voices full of love and laughter.

On the other end of the emotional scale was a family or girlfriend saying goodbye to a young soldier, sailor, or marine before he boarded the train. From their expressions, it was clear that some of them were afraid this would be their final farewell. Pretending to look at her magazine, June watched one young couple kissing and embracing. The girl was crying and holding onto her soldier, as if by sheer force she could keep him with her. As the train whistle sounded and the conductor shouted, "All aboard!" he slowly disentangled himself and headed for the open door of the train car. Resolutely looking every inch a strong brave soldier, with his ramrod straight posture and strong jutting chin, no one would have known this parting was as difficult for him as the girl he was leaving behind. Only June, watching, saw a tear threaten to escape from his eye.

This scene, and what greeted them when they stepped onto the train, again brought the reality of war closer to them. The car was full of soldiers, sailors, and marines milling about in the aisle or sitting on their suitcases. These were young men on their way to camp, some for more training and others to a point of embarkation to someplace overseas.

Women, mostly young, some with babies or small children, occupied most of the seats. They were either traveling to or home from the base where their husbands were stationed. Difficult though it was for Polly, June, and Cecil to get through the corridor, Polly had traveled by train since she was a child, and was undaunted by the lack of seating. "Come on," she commanded, "Follow me. There have to be three seats somewhere on this train." Having said this she led them from car to car.

Whistles and calls of "Hi, Blondie" and "Hi, Carrot Top" followed them as they maneuvered their way through the maze of men crowding the aisles. June's cheeks turned red, but secretly she enjoyed it, but Polly wasn't amused. After all, June wasn't quite fourteen.

They finally found three seats together. Occupying the other one was a young woman holding a baby on her lap. Talking to her, they found this truly was a small world. She was on her way to join her soldier husband at Camp Aberdeen, the camp Burrel had helped build when they lived at Bush River Inn.

June and Polly were happy to hold the baby, giving the young mother a respite to relax or move around the train. She was anxious to hear all about the area around Aberdeen, and they enjoyed reminiscing about the time they'd spent there.

Since the camp was so close to Washington, they told her she shouldn't miss at least one trip there. "Since we left they've been building a new monument, the Jefferson Memorial," June said. "I heard on the radio it's going to be finished this year. Maybe you can get to see it."

From the yearning in June's voice, it was obvious she was sorry she was going to miss it. Smiling, Polly told their new friend about June and Cecil's ventures into the city and how much they had enjoyed it. "How long are you going to be in Maryland?" Polly asked. "Is your husband going to be stationed there long?"

With a glance at the sign on the wall at the end of the corridor, "Loose lips sink ships," she murmured, "I really can't say. My husband says they won't know when or where they're going. The government doesn't want to take any chances the information will reach the wrong ears." Smiling sympathetically, Polly couldn't help feel a sense of relief that Burrel's age and the children kept him from being drafted. She and their seatmate must be close to the same age.

A carnival air prevailed during the afternoon and evening as they could hear the banter of the men seated in the aisles, feel the swaying movement of the train as the wheels clacked away the miles, and hear the sound of the whistle as they passed through towns or crossed highways.

The young men took pleasure in flirting with June and watching Polly's flustered mother hen reaction. They laughed when she flounced out of her seat and made June change places and sit by the window.

The overcrowding in the train made it impossible for all to eat in the dining car. To compensate, a white-coated man, carrying a tray, walked through the cars hawking sandwiches, apples, potato chips and other snacks. His call of, "Get your hot dogs and soft drinks here!" brought calls of, "When's the ball game starting?" This was followed by more laughter.

Looking first at them, then at Cecil, Polly thought of how little difference there was between their ages, she fervently prayed these light hearted young men would all return safely, and that this war would be over before Cecil was old enough to be drafted.

~

When night came, the conductor turned the lights low and the hubbub of the day diminished as people tried to sleep in their seats. Gazing out the window at the star filled sky and the lights from an occasional farmhouse, June could hear the hushed voices and the sound of someone quietly playing a harmonica.

Too excited to fall asleep, her mind wandered to the letters she had received a few days ago. One was from Ramon, who much to her surprise, had turned out to be a prolific letter writer. Joy and Nadia, Miss Phoebe, and Miss Jane all were there beside her as she mentally reread the letters she had memorized. Sometimes she was homesick to see them, but now, on this trip, she had a deep, unexplainable feeling that going to Newark was going home.

This was strange, since she'd only visited and never actually lived there, unless you counted the brief period in her mother's womb, before her parents had embarked on their West Virginia venture. Maybe this feeling persisted because her dad was already in Ohio, and home for her was wherever he was. "Going home, going home," the rhythm of the wheels seemed to be saying. Every mile was bringing her closer to him and to her mother and little brother. Could she dare to hope that after close to two and a half years, she and Cecil would see them again?

As the train traveled through a small city, lighted homes and factories flashed by. She glimpsed night workers, carrying lunch boxes, streaming in through the open doors of a defense plant. She wondered if these factories were like the ones where her mother or her stepfather, Bill, worked. It was hard for her to picture her mother in those surroundings.

The mental images she had were of her mother in the kitchen, or in the yard working in her flowerbeds, or selling tickets at the cavern office. Sitting at a bench, checking shell casings didn't fit into that image. Nor could she picture her mother, Bill, and Dickie as a family, although realistically she knew they were as much one as she, Cecil, her dad, and Polly.

She had always tried not to allow herself to miss them, but here in the near silence of this train car, bringing her ever closer, she relaxed her guard and felt overwhelmed with the sense of loss. Taking her mother's letter from her pocket, she held it close to her face, because sometimes she thought she could catch a whiff of the almost forgotten scent of her perfume.

Looking around and seeing that almost everyone around her was asleep, and those awake seemed lost in their own thoughts, she opened the letter and by the dim overhead light reread parts of it.

Almost as clearly as watching the scene unfold on a movie screen, her mother's words painted pictures so vividly that June could feel herself as an invisible audience watching as they went about their daily lives.

She smiled to herself when she read about her little brother selling newspapers on the street corner. She could see him going to The News Journal office for his papers, and then standing on the corner by the banks hawking them. "News Journal! News Journal! Read all about it! Canned Goods and Shoes Rationed! Eisenhower Named Supreme Commander of Allied Forces!"

Her mother had said Dickie had that corner to himself on weekdays, but every Friday a man named Fischer sat up his news cart there and chased him away. Young as he was, Dickie wouldn't admit defeat. He'd just take his papers and move a few feet away. June smiled at the image of this skinny, freckle faced boy, her little brother, with the newspaper carrier bag thrown over his shoulder, continuing business as usual. As her mother had said, "He just hollered even louder to attract his customer's attention."

"Good for him," she thought. "Why couldn't that grown man find his own corner and leave my little brother alone?"

As she drifted off to sleep, her last thought was of Dickie selling all his papers, and with his moneybag full, going home to the apartment he, his mom and Bill shared. She wondered if she would ever visit it, other than in her mind?

In the morning she woke to the sound of the baby crying and the ruckus caused by people talking in the background as the hawker moved through the aisle yelling, "Hot coffee, milk and donuts. Get your breakfast here." The din was less as people settled down to eat the meager fare.

Cecil had been enjoying the trip, sitting up part of the night playing cards with some of the soldiers. So far it had been interesting. He'd been amused by the soldiers flirting with his sister. The ones he'd told had been chagrined to learn her age, but that hadn't stopped them from talking to her. "They must be practicing for when they meet someone their own age," he thought as he gulped down his third donut.

"I'll sure be glad when we get there," he told Polly. "I'm ready for some real food." He brightened visibly when she told him that he'd only have to eat one more meal on the train. They'd be getting into Newark early in the afternoon.

As the day wore on, stiff and sore from sitting so long, the passengers left their seats to move. Walking down the corridor while the train swayed from side to side was fun and exciting, and helped pass the time. Polly, June, and Cecil were almost too excited to sit still. They were almost there, and Burrel would be waiting for them.

CHAPTER FOURTEEN

HOME AT LAST

It seemed like forever before they heard the long anticipated announcement, "Next stop Newark!" As soon as they did, June and Cecil started to stand up, ready to go, but Polly stopped them. "Hold on," she said. "You might as well sit down. We're almost there, but not quite. They always announce a station miles before they get there."

Impatiently they sat and waited. Soon they were passing houses and business buildings. "Is this it? Are we in Newark?" June asked, as she noticed other passengers reaching for their overhead luggage.

"This is it!" Polly exclaimed excitedly. "Grab the bags and we'll be ready when we pull into the station." As they could feel the train slowing, they were ready with bags in hand to rush out the door when it came to a stop.

Straining to look through the window, they could see a crowd of people of all ages standing on the platform. When they went through the door, the scene that greeted them was a replica of what they'd seen the day before. Loved ones in Newark were as enthusiastically greeting their young returning servicemen as the ones in Mississippi had greeted theirs.

Looking around, a baffled June murmured, "Dad's not here! I was sure he'd meet us." Over the sound of her disappointed voice, they heard their names being called. "Polly, June, Cecil, over here."

As they looked around for the source of the voice, a large group of people surged forward to greet a returning sailor. This made it possible for them to see Burrel, waving his arm to get their attention. By his grin and the sparkle in his eyes, it was obvious he was as happy to see them as they were to see him.

They'd hardly had time to greet each other when Cecil said, "Okay. Let's get some real food!" While Polly explained what they'd had to eat, Burrel steered them to the car and headed a couple blocks uptown to the lunch counter at Woolworth's. Wolfing down a cheeseburger, French fries and a milkshake, Cecil announced, "This is more like it!"

"Some things never change," Burrel laughingly exclaimed. "It's good to have you all home." Nodding her agreement, June was hoping this was going to be home for a long time to come. She was ready to stay in one place for awhile. From the expression on her father's face, he seemed to feel the same way.

While the adults lingered over their coffee, June and Cecil glanced around the store and out the window. The store and sidewalks were crowded with a mixture of town people and farmers. "Saturdays are always like this," Burrel explained. "When we go out, check out the cars parked around the square. A lot of them will have people sitting in them, just watching other people go by. It's a regular Saturday pastime for some people."

On a much smaller scale, the activity reminded them of the hustle and bustle they'd noticed when they'd been in Baltimore. The apparent difference here was that people seemed to know each other. This was evident by the number of people who stopped at the counter to talk to Burrel.

As they walked back to the car June looked around at the wide streets and the tall stately courthouse surrounded by its tree shaded lawn. All of this, she later learned was called the courthouse square. Department stores, men and women's clothing shops, a couple five and ten cent stores, an equal number of dollar stores, a hotel, restaurants, drugstores and theaters stood side by side on the four streets that formed this square.

Backing out of the diagonal parking space, Burrel commented to Polly, "Driving around this square is as bad as driving in Washington. When you start driving around it, you'll see that there's not a single traffic light or white line. It's every man for himself."

As he was talking, June and Cecil, sitting in the back seat, watched cars switching lanes, darting in front of them as if trying to escape from this confusing maze to one of the four wide streets that led away from the courthouse square. "They remind me of the dodge'um cars we drove at the fair," June said as one narrowly missed hitting their side fender. Cecil agreed, but he couldn't help think this was as dangerous as riding with Polly while she was learning to drive.

Burrel managed to exit onto East Main Street without being struck by another car. "I've been staying with Mace and Mabel, and we'll be staying there tonight," he said. "I have the trailer parked in their back yard, but since there's no way we can hook up to the water and electricity, we can't live in it. We'll start looking for a house of our own tomorrow. I didn't do it sooner as I wanted you all to help pick one out."

～

This was news to June and Cecil. They had naturally assumed they would be living in the trailer. June was too excited at the prospect of spending time with Rose to ask any more questions, although it seemed strange to her they would be looking for a house when they had their home on wheels.

That evening the mystery was solved when June overheard Polly telling Mabel that one day, when they had first gotten to Mississippi, she had discovered something that upset her while she was cleaning the trailer. When she'd lifted the top of the stove to clean under the burners she'd found the remains of an old dried up fried potato. Since she hadn't fried potatoes since they'd bought the trailer, she had realized they weren't its first occupants.

She and Burrel had been understandably upset, since they'd paid the price of a new trailer on one that was obviously used. Further examination revealed other evidence to support her suspicions. Burrel had immediately contacted the dealer and was now in the process of negotiating some sort of price adjustment. If the dealer wasn't willing to do that, then he was demanding the trailer be picked up and their money refunded.

June and Cecil were both pleased to hear Polly say, "I think, whatever they do about the trailer, it's time we moved into a house. These kids need more room. Besides, it's about time they had some stability in their lives. They haven't complained, but it's hard on them moving from place to place."

Finding a house was easier said than done. The first few newspaper ads Polly answered, she was told emphatically that they didn't rent to people with children, because they were too destructive. June and Cecil were both indignant, first at being considered children and second at the thought that children would be allowed to destroy anyone's property. The very idea was against every thing they'd ever been taught. In both their minds they could picture themselves living at the cavern and hear their mother telling them, "You are to treat everyone else's property with as much respect as you do your very own."

Surprisingly, the solution to their housing problem was close at hand. Mace and Mabel's next door neighbors, the McPherson's, had fixed up a three bedroom upstairs apartment in their home. It was empty and for rent. Being in a private home, it wasn't ideal, but since they didn't want to wear out their welcome at Mace and Mabel's, they decided to take it. Once they had moved in, it didn't take them long to find that Mrs. McPherson considered herself a private eye, and June and Cecil were the prime targets of her snooping. Whether she was checking to see how long they left the water running or spying on them and their friends, she practiced her second profession, reporting.

Anytime Polly or Burrel returned from an outing, they were met at the door by Mrs. McPherson and a barrage of complaints, "June ran up the stairs. We could hear her from where we were sitting in the living room. Cecil and his friends were laughing and making noise. June let the water run when she washed the dishes." Pursing her lips, she added, "You're going to have to do something about those children."

At first Polly listened politely, but the pettiness of the complaints finally got to her, causing her to coolly say, "Now let me get this straight. I'm to tell them, no laughing, only tiptoeing up and down the steps, and June should wash the dishes in a tea cup of water. Would there be anything else? How about breathing? Does that bother you, too?"

As Mrs. McPherson flounced back into her apartment, Polly muttered, "Busy body, Old Biddy." Then she stomped up the steps to tell June and Cecil of this newest encounter. June was furious. "You know what else she did? When Butch and I came home from the movies the other night, we were saying goodnight, and there she stood, looking out the glass in the door at us. She wasn't a foot from where we were standing. She turned away when Butch smiled and said hi to her."

"Good for him!" Polly said. This boy was the first one June had ever had a real date with, and it was obvious she had been embarrassed by the landlady's behavior. "Your dad and I are going to have to talk about this when he gets home. We need to do something about it."

Since the dealer had made a slight adjustment in the price of the trailer and they had subsequently sold it, this left them without a readily available place to live. They didn't feel quite as independent as they had been.

"Moving out of the trailer was to give June and Cecil a better place to live," Polly told Burrel that evening. "This isn't better. In fact it's worse."

After hearing about the newest bout of their landlady's complaints, he asked, "Is she right? Are the kids making too much noise? If they are, I'll give them a talking to."

Imagining June or Cecil getting one of his "talking tos" Polly was glad she could honestly reply, "No, they're not. In my opinion she shouldn't even be renting out these rooms. She listens for every little sound, and if she doesn't hear anything, she'll creep up the steps to see what she's missing. The other day I was in the kitchen. It was so hot I'd stripped down to my slip while I was ironing. I heard a noise in the hall, and I almost jumped out of my skin when I turned around and saw her standing there looking in the door."

Burrel laughed as he pictured the scene before saying, "I guess living in a private home isn't the answer. What I'd really like to do is buy a house. The job at the aluminum plant is going to last for awhile, and when it ends I think I can find other work around here. If we can get one with a low enough down payment, I think I can swing it. What do you think?" he asked anxiously. "How does a home of our own sound to you?"

"That sounds good, but I don't actually think we'll find what we want right away. I really don't want to stay here any longer. June is really upset, and I think it's beginning to get to Cecil," she replied. "There are some new apartments on Union Street. I'll take the bus over there tomorrow and check them out. What do you think?" she asked. He readily agreed and she and June happily made plans for their apartment hunting expedition.

When he got home from work the next evening, they met him at the door and excitedly told him what they'd found out. "They have a nice apartment on the second floor. It's furnished with new furniture. Everything in it is new, but best of all it's private," Polly told him.

When she added that it rented for fifty-five dollars a month, he agreed it might be just what they were looking for. "What do you think of it?" he asked June.

"I love it," she said enthusiastically. "Mom didn't tell you, but all the furniture is blonde. It's so modern! It's really groovy!" Burrel smiled at her description. It had taken awhile to get used to some of her slang, but he'd learned when she called something groovy, that meant it was wonderful, the best.

"Do you want to go over tomorrow and rent it?" he asked Polly. "If you and June like it that much, then I don't have to see it. Cecil and I will leave it up to the two of you," he added.

Giving Mrs. McPherson notice and moving to their new home was accomplished in a matter of days. For June this was a good move as she had just gone to work baby sitting a little boy and girl for a young couple. They lived in one of the few houses located outside Newark on Route 79, just south of the city limits.

If she'd been able to predict the future, she'd have seen the city of Heath with its houses, schools, shopping center, many businesses and the county's first mall spring up around that little house. Strictly in the country though, that summer of nineteen forty-three, the little white house and a few farmhouses were the only ones for miles along that lonely two lane stretch of highway. Part of the condition of her employment was that she had to be on duty twenty-four hours a day five days a week. Every Sunday evening June's dad would drop her off. He'd return to pick her up the following Saturday morning.

Her employers, Mr. and Mrs. Worth, worked the swing shift at Owens Corning Fiberglass in Newark, leaving June alone to care for six-year-old Butch and his four-year-old sister Beth. Since the parents worked rotating shifts, they were either working or sleeping during the day, giving June almost total responsibility for the little ones.

It was hard for her to think of this as work, since she immediately fell in love with the children. She thoroughly enjoyed the hours she spent reading to them and playing games. Since the MacDonald farm was just down the road, she would sing "Old MacDonald Had A Farm" with Butch and Beth laughing as they all made the animals sounds together. June was a combination playmate and little mother to them. Occasionally she would take them by bus to the playground at White's Field.

No matter what they were doing when the noise from the traffic signaled that the construction workers from the aluminum plant were going home they would sit on the front porch and watch for her dad's car. As the tan and brown Chevrolet with him at the wheel drove by, they'd all shout and wave until the car was out of sight.

Not being clairvoyant, she couldn't know that not only her dad, the most important man in her present life, but a stranger who would be the most important one in her future also passed the little house every day.

Having just graduated from high school and working at The Aluminum Plant that summer as a carpenter's assistant while waiting to be drafted, this dark haired young man, her future husband, would have considered thirteen year old June a mere child. Even if he had seen her, he wouldn't have given her a second glance. That was no longer the case when after the war was over, they finally met.

Going home on the weekend, she soon discovered what the rest of the family already knew. There was a major flaw in their lovely new upstairs apartment. The temperature was as close to Hades as they ever hoped to be. No matter how lovely the rooms and furniture were, that couldn't make up for the discomfort from the stifling heat.

They had also soon found the disadvantage of not having a yard and shade trees. June and her cousin Rose, her constant weekend visitor, managed to compensate by sitting on the fire escape landing trying to catch a slight breeze and escape from the heat. Many times they would stay there talking into the wee hours of the morning.

"Have you ever been to Mansfield?" June asked Rose during one of their late night gabfests. When Rose replied that she never had, June continued, "I know it's not very far, but you'd think it was a thousand miles the way everyone around here acts. I don't know why Mom doesn't come down to see us. It's been almost three years since we saw her."

"Have you said anything to your dad about it?" Rose asked. "If you haven't, I think it's time you did." Even at her young age, Rose was pretty independent and direct, and she couldn't understand what was keeping June from seeing her mother if she wanted to.

"Dad doesn't like to talk about it, and I don't want to upset him. Mom said she's working on it. She knows how much I want to see Mom and Dickie, but Mom is still afraid Dad will try to take Dickie away from her. It's a real mess."

"Calling Polly and your Mom both "Mom" is really confusing," Rose replied. "I guess you're saying Polly is working on it. Doesn't it confuse you having two moms?" Rose asked.

"It might if I ever got to see my real mom again, but at this point I've only had one for the last couple years." Sighing deeply, June said, "I might as well be in Mississippi for all the good it does me." Rose was the only one June confided in about these feelings. "I just have to be patient," she said. "I know eventually, Mom and Dad will get it worked out."

In response Rose rolled her big brown eyes and exclaimed, "I certainly hope so!" Then changing the subject, she asked "Do you want to go to the movies tomorrow? Casablanca is on with Humphrey Bogart and Ingrid Bergman."

Since walking downtown and going to the movies were two of their favorite activities, June didn't need to be coaxed. The attraction at the theater wasn't just the movie playing, but the air conditioning. An advertisement proclaiming, "It's cool inside," always shared top billing with the most exciting movies and the most glamorous movie stars.

A trip downtown wasn't complete without a stop at Gallegher's Drug Store's soda fountain for a banana split or at The Chatterbox for a frosted malt. This concoction, a cross between a malted milk shake and soft ice cream was the specialty of the house and had caused The Chatterbox to become a hangout for teenagers.

～

One weekend when June came home from her job, her dad and Polly were discussing buying a house. The discussion was almost to the point of turning into an argument. Burrel was in favor of buying the house, and Polly was objecting. "Now tell me," he said, "What's wrong with it?"

"What's wrong with it?" she repeated. "For one thing it's too big. For another, it's across the street from your brother. I'm not sure I want to live that close to my in-laws."

He knew she liked small, cozy houses, but the one they were discussing only had six rooms. With the four of them, that didn't seem too big to him, and he put all his powers of persuasion into trying to convince her. "Honey," he coaxed, "Just think about it. We need at least three bedrooms, and that's what that house has. When the kids start bringing their friends home, it's not going to seem too big at all. As for living close to Mace, if I ever have to work out of town I'd feel better knowing he and Mabel would be close. They could help you if you ever needed anything."

Polly reluctantly agreed to think about it. By the time June came home the following weekend, the decision had been made. If they could arrange the financing, they would be owners of their first house.

Walking through it the first time, the feeling of coming home that June had felt when they first arrived in Newark, returned. Only this time it was much stronger. Breathing a sigh of relief that this was a home without wheels, she dared to hope that they were finally putting down roots, that she wouldn't soon hear the dreaded words "We're moving!" For the first time since they'd embarked on their vagabond existence, she felt, "This is it. We're home."

She liked everything about the first floor, the small front porch, the spacious entrance hall, the wide floor boards in the airy living room, the ceramic tile rimming the corner fireplace, the sun streaming through the tall wide windows in the dining room, and the white cabinets lining one wall in the kitchen.

Climbing the open staircase to the upstairs, she was again in a wide hall with rooms fanning out on all sides. When she walked into the front bedroom her eyes immediately went to the two large windows. Peering through them she could see her uncle's house across the street. She was pleasantly surprised when she realized that the window to Rose's room was directly across from where she was standing. "This could be fun!" she thought.

Turning her attention away from the view from the window, she spent a few minutes examining her surroundings. The wide gleaming floorboards and the tiny flower print design on the wallpaper seemed to add to the room's feeling of spaciousness. To make the room perfect in her teenaged eyes, there was not just one, but there were two walk-in closets. She couldn't believe her eyes. "Two closets and all this space," she marveled. "It is beautiful," she sighed softly. It truly was the room of her dreams!

Since she had already made up her mind this was to be hers, she was glad to hear Cecil lay claim to the back bedroom. Not quite as large as the front room, and with only one closet, it offered something, though, that instantly appealed to him. A tree stood on a slight embankment with its wide branches touching the window panes. It offered all kinds of opportunities to a young man ready to assert his independence.

Between their two rooms were the guest room and the bathroom. Burrel and Polly were going to use the dining room for their bedroom. Polly had only agreed to buy the house if he'd assent to that arrangement. Her loathing of big houses was equaled only by her dislike of stairs.

While Polly wasn't happy with the size or location, June loved it. The spaciousness after living cooped up in a minuscule trailer, and being so close to Rose, her best friend, made it perfect. Even though this house would hold much joy for the family, it would also witness much unhappiness and sorrow. For now though, it was full of excitement and anticipation.

Since the furniture in the trailer was built in and the apartments they'd had were furnished, they found themselves with a large empty house. They couldn't move in until they bought some furniture. The planning and shopping was the one aspect about this move Polly enjoyed, as it gave her a chance to indulge her passion for maple. She furnished the living room with a couch and two chairs with maple frames and overstuffed cushions, and a matching coffee table and end tables.

Using the same theme, she helped June pick out a Jenny Lind style bed, a dresser, and an unfinished vanity and bench. Using the talents she'd developed to make June clothes, she stitched together a red and white checked gingham ruffled bedspread and vanity skirt. If June had liked the room before, she now loved it.

To save money, Polly shopped around in used furniture stores where she was able to find a white painted wooden kitchen table and chairs. Months later, watching Cecil finish a special project on that table, she was glad she hadn't bought the maple one she'd had her eye on.

~

Working now, and getting old enough to drive, Cecil had been looking around for a car. He'd seen an ad in the paper for an English Austin for sale in Zanesville. Since he was limited by funds and the wartime automobile shortage, the price was low enough to appeal to him. Burrel was out of town, but Uncle Mace agreed to take him and his friend Phil Haas to check it out.

When they found the address and knocked on the door, the owner warmly greeted them and nodded for them to follow him around the outside of the house. Leading them to a barn-like garage, he pointed to the Austin. Cecil, Phil, and Mace stood with their mouths agape. There was no car, only a frame with all its inner parts scattered from one end of the room to the other.

"What is this? Your ad said you had a car for sale!" Cecil exclaimed. "You didn't say anything about it being in pieces." Mace and Phil nodded their agreement.

The car's owner grinned and said, "If you're the least bit mechanical, you can put it together. As far as I know all the parts are here. If I have to put it together, the price will go up. You wouldn't want that to happen would you?"

Phil pulled Cecil over to the side and told him, "I'm mechanical. I think I can help you put this thing together. He's right. You will never find another at this price. If we can't do it, you can find someone else to buy it."

Though not wildly enthusiastic, Cecil finally agreed to buy it. Loading the parts onto Mace's truck, they returned to Newark where the purchase was greeted with dismay. "That's a car?" June asked, and Polly echoed her sentiments.

Their reaction strengthened Cecil and Phil's resolve to make it work. As they spread the parts out in the garage, Phil said, "I think we can get Johnny Bracken to help us. He knows something about cars too."

All their spare time went into the project. While sorting the pieces, they encountered their first problem. The timing gear was missing. After trying unsuccessfully to find one in Columbus and Zanesville, they were about ready to give up until someone told them about a place in Newark where almost any mechanical part could be found. Skepticism was showing on their faces when they sauntered into the store and asked if they had a timing gear. Their attitude quickly changed at the proprietor's matter of fact response to their inquiry, "Sure, we do."

Timing gear in hand, they returned triumphantly to Lawrence Street and embarked on their project. The garage, which was built into the embankment next to the house, had makeshift benches against each wall. They served as an assembly line for the three young men. Although it took them months of trial and error, they did succeed in turning these buckets of parts into a functioning automobile.

Their efforts drew the attention of Herb and Kenny Channel who lived across the street, a few houses from Mace and Mabel's house. Close to Cecil's age they had quickly become close friends. Although they didn't know anything about automobiles, they would often be at the garage observing the progress.

One Saturday when June and Polly came home from the grocery store, they found the project had been moved into the house. Looking like a grotesque gray centerpiece, the carburetor, surrounded by other automotive parts, rested on the kitchen table. Burrel, Cecil, and Phil with tools in hand were peering at it while the Channel boys were standing behind them looking on.

They were too absorbed in their project to hear June and Polly come in. Polly quickly got their attention, though, with her explosive outcry, "What in the name of heaven is going on here?" Startled, every eye turned to look at her. Phil and the Channel boys' looks of astonishment contrasted with Cecil and Burrel's sheepish expressions.

While she stood hands on her hips, glaring at them, Cecil muttered, "Ah, Mom," and Burrel softly declared, "Honey, the boys needed more light to work on the carburetor, so I told them they could bring it in here." The withering look she gave him was enough for him to fear this wouldn't be the last he'd hear about it.

As the day wore on, the boys' good humor proved contagious, and she soon joined in their good natured bantering. Burrel grinned as he sipped coffee and watched the interaction. She returned his grin and patted him on the shoulder as she moved about the kitchen, putting the groceries away and preparing lunch. He breathed a sigh of relief as he realized her anger had been short lived. His grin widened as it struck him this night he'd been anticipating all week, wasn't going to be ruined after all.

~

    Saturday night was their time to be alone. June and Rose usually went to the movies, and Cecil and his friends could be counted on to be out of the house for hours. Practically newlyweds, he and Polly had no problem finding something to do for the few hours they'd have the house to themselves. Closing the wide double doors that separated their bedroom from the living room, assured their privacy. If either June or Cecil came home early and saw the closed doors, it was as effective as hanging a "Do Not Disturb" sign on the door knob.

    When either of the children was out late, Polly would leave a lamp lit in the entrance hall. Its light cast a soft glow, illuminating the living room, clearly showing the position of the double doors. A squeaking board on the front porch, coupled with the opening of the front door would usually signal their arrival home and would elicit an inquiry from the bedroom of, "Which one of you is it?"

    Especially if the double doors were open, there was no sneaking in past curfew. June had found out the hard way once when she'd gotten home from a date past her eleven o'clock curfew. She had been greeted by her angry mother who ordered her and Butch inside, and vehemently scolded them both. She had firmly informed the shaken boy that if he wanted to take June out again, he would have to have her home on time. June hadn't expected to ever see him again, but he not only came back, but never missed getting her home before curfew. Not wanting a repeat of that incident from then on, June kept her eyes on the clock.

    For Cecil, this was a different matter. He'd soon learned to look in through the living room window before coming in. If the doors were closed, he knew neither of them would hear him. If they were open, he'd slip around to the back of the house, shimmy up the tree trunk, scoot across the thick limb that brushed against his bedroom window, and silently ease his way into the room. No one was ever the wiser.

At least that was what he thought during the summer. When winter came he tried it once too often. He was going to school and was employed as a laborer at the railroad yards. Since he was working like an adult, he felt he was entitled to some adult vices, mainly drinking beer.

After one such Friday night with his friends, past midnight, he slipped in through his window and promptly fell asleep. When the alarm wakened him the next morning, he turned it off, and settled under the covers determined to stay there. Before he could again fall asleep, he became aware of a pounding on the door followed by his dad's voice saying, "It's time to get up, Son."

His aching head felt as big as a balloon. The sounds coming from the other side of the door seemed like an entire drum corps was marching back and forth across his skull. "I'm not going to work today," he said. "I don't feel well."

"If you felt good enough to stay out half the night, you can go to work today," his dad firmly replied. "Now get up and come downstairs." The tone of his father's voice was enough to convince him, it would do no good to argue. Crawling from under the warmth of the covers, he shuffled downstairs, ate breakfast, and reluctantly made his way to the railroad yards.

Inhaling the frigid air helped wake him, but nothing eased his aching head. He groaned when he was directed to a box car, handed a shovel, and told to empty all the coal onto the ground. Even without the hangover, the job wouldn't have been easy, since the coal had gotten wet and was frozen.

Before he could shovel any of it, he had to first loosen it with a pick. Every time he brought the pick down on the frozen coal, pain would jolt through his head. Moaning and muttering, "Oh, no," it took him all day to empty the freight car. One thing he'd learned that day was that it was no fun to have a hangover. With every shovelful he became more resolved to put his drinking days behind him.

He never found out whether his dad knew about his hangover or the use he'd made of the tree. Neither one ever mentioned it. Although he never gave up using his special private entrance, he was more determined than ever not to be heard. He succeeded so well that June, sleeping across the hall, seldom heard him come in.

During that first summer in Newark, June's feeling that the move to Newark was a homecoming seemed to grow. The house, her room, time spent with Rose becoming acquainted with the world around them added to that feeling.

While Cecil and his friends had spent time reassembling the car, she and Rose had explored every inch of the town. One day Rose showed her Lincoln School, and another time they walked downtown and checked out the high school. The few blocks she and Rose would have to walk to Lincoln weren't nearly as far as the mile and a half Cecil and Inez would have to go to the high school.

Rose introduced June to Herb and Kenny Channel's sister Betty. A petite blue eyed blonde, she elicited envy in both June and Rose: first for her collection of angora sweaters her grandmother had bought her, and second, because she was old enough to go to dances at the USO, a war time organization set up for service men and women. All June and Rose knew about it was that once a week dances were held and girls were invited to attend. Like everything else about this war, they were too young to be part of it.

Many times, seeing them sitting on the porch on her way home, Betty would stop and tell them about her evening. She was a friendly vivacious girl and despite the difference in their ages, she and June became friends.

One night when June was spending the night with Rose, Aunt Mabel overheard them talking about their plans for the next day. "You're going to Moundbuilder's Park?" she asked.

"I thought we might take the bus out there and walk around the mounds," Rose replied, referring to the circular Indian mounds located at the edge of town. "There's not much else to do there, but I thought June might enjoy it."

"That's all there is to do there now, but before you girls were born, it was a different matter," she said. Turning to June, she continued, "When we first moved here, it was a county fairgrounds. Mace and I went there a couple times with your mom and dad back when they were courting."

The mention of her mom startled June as no one in the family ever referred to her. It was almost as if she were dead or had never existed.

Seemingly unaware of June's reaction, her aunt's eyes sparkled and her face was bathed in smiles when she continued her story. "The summer before Burrel and Priscilla were married, Priscilla and I had been coaxing Burrel and Mace to take us to the county fair, but they didn't seem to be too interested. We found it hard to believe they didn't want to go, as they'd always liked such things. Besides the rides and food on the midway, there was going to be horse racing inside the circle mound."

"Priscilla loved corn dogs, and about the only place you could buy one was at the fair. Since Burrel hardly ever denied her anything, she was understandably upset." Silent for a moment, as if gathering her thoughts, Mabel smiled and continued, "I finally got it out of Mace, that with the cost of courting, Burrel didn't have the money for their tickets. He could afford the food, but not the food and admission."

"I don't know whose idea it was to sneak in, but that's just what we did!" she exclaimed. Too caught up in the past to notice the shocked faces of her audience, she went on, "We drove to the back of the park and climbed over the fence. It was too dark for anyone to notice us. Once we got over the fence, we blended in with the crowd, and no one paid any attention to us."

"I'll never forget that night," she sighed. "We had a great time. Priscilla got her corn dog, and we rode all the rides and watched the horse races." Glancing at June's rapt face, she went on, "Your Mom's conscience bothered her afterwards, and she told Burrel she'd never do anything like that again. Everyone was disappointed because we'd had so much fun that we all wanted to go back the next night."

"Did you?" June asked. Her aunt chuckled as she replied, "We sure did! I don't know how they did it, but the fellows came up with the money for tickets for Priscilla and me. Since they didn't go in with us, I guess they must have gone over the fence again, because they joined us in a few minutes."

While June and Rose watched Mabel's smiling face and twinkling eyes, as she relived this episode from the past, it was hard to picture their parents as the carefree young people she was talking about. "Boy, Dad would give me a good talking to if I ever pulled anything like that!" June exclaimed.

A slight blush covered Mabel's round cheeks at June's remark. As pillars of the church, she and Mace were strict with their own children.

Maybe she'd made a mistake telling the girls, but she'd been too caught up in her memories to give a thought to what they might think. "Oh, well," she mused, "It doesn't hurt once in awhile for them to know their parents were young too. I think I'll remind Mace and Burrel. Maybe it'll make Mace loosen up a little."

THE CIRCLE MENDED

CHAPTER FIFTEEN
THE LONG AWAITED REUNION

Lying in bed that night, June's mind replayed the picture of the young Priscilla and Burrel, laughing, having a good time. As the images flickered across her mind, other memories intruded, of herself and her brothers as young children living in the cavern house, playing in the field, silently following the guide through the cavern, hurrying home from school to listen to Jack Armstrong, All American Boy. In the center of all these memories was her mother, smiling, loving, always there.

These memories brought her an almost unbearable sense of loss. She knew that particular part of her life was over; the family she was envisioning no longer existed and never would again. Still, she and her mother were little more than fifty miles apart. Why couldn't they see each other? For the thousandth time she wondered if somehow she had been to blame for her mother leaving. That night she dreamed about her. This only served to strengthen her resolve that, once again, they were going to be together.

Knowing how June felt, Polly talked about it to Burrel the next night as part of their pillow talk. The very thought of Priscilla coming to his home to see the children brought back all the hurt and bitterness he thought he'd managed to erase. "I'm not the only one involved in this," he said. "Priscilla won't let me see Dickie. If she wants to see June and Cecil, then she has to give a little too."

Exasperated, Polly exclaimed, "Listen to yourself! You two are acting more like children than your offspring are! Just because you and Priscilla couldn't get along doesn't mean everyone else has to suffer. I don't think it's bothering Cecil, but June is miserable about it."

"I know," he mumbled. "Priscilla thinks that if she lets Dickie come see me, I'll keep him. How do I know she wouldn't try to keep June and Cecil?"

"For crying out loud!" Polly raged. "I'm going in on the couch. There's not room enough for me, you, and Priscilla in this bed!" Pillow in hand, she flounced into the living room and sank down on the couch where she sat smoking and fuming about their disagreement. "Old Bull Head," she muttered.

Stretching his long undershirt to cover his bare lower body, he followed and settled himself next to her. "What do you mean saying Priscilla is in bed with us? You're the one who brought it up. When do I ever talk about her?"

"You don't have to. I just feel sometimes that she's there between us. At times you're so quiet, I wonder if you're thinking about her." Putting his strong arm around her, smiling gently, and explaining in a calm soothing voice that Priscilla was in the past, and she was his present and future, caused her anger to dissipate.

Traipsing behind him into their bedroom, she couldn't contain a giggle as she said, "Honey, if you want to hide everything, you're going to have to get some longer undershirts." From his whoop of laughter and the closed double doors, it was obvious there would be no more arguing, at least, not that night.

Tired of waiting for the adults to make a decision, June finally decided she wasn't going to wait any longer. Over Sunday breakfast she confronted her father, "Dad, I want to see Mom and Dickie. We've been here for a couple months, and I think its time we either went to see her, or she and Dickie came to see us."

The determined look on his daughter's face stopped him before he could again offer an excuse to postpone the meeting. Looking from June to Cecil, he remembered how patient they had been with their vagabond existence for these last years. Neither had complained, but June was making it clear that was no longer going to be the case.

He was quiet for so long, June was beginning to think he wasn't going to answer her. So many thoughts were running through his mind. When and where should this meeting take place? If Priscilla came here would Bill be with her? Would Priscilla finally let him see Dickie? Should he keep her from seeing June and Cecil if she wouldn't let him see Dickie? Was he being selfish? Was his own bitterness keeping him from considering his children's needs?

"You're going to have to give me time to see what I can do," he said. "Your Mom and I will need to talk this over," he added, referring to Polly. "Then I guess I'll have to see what Priscilla has to say about it." Sighing heavily, he got up from the table and walked out on the porch where he sat quietly smoking and thinking. Handing him a fresh cup of coffee, Polly joined him. Pulling her chair close to him, they sat talking all morning.

When June walked by them on her way across the street to see Rose, their conversation stopped, but her dad did smile his encouragement. "I think I'm going to get to see Mom and Dickie," June excitedly told Rose. "That's what Mom and Dad are talking about now."

At dinner Burrel informed her of his decision. "June," he said. "You can write your mother and ask her to come see you and Cecil. You can tell her if she comes down the next couple weekends that I won't be here. I have to work overtime."

Although she had told Rose she thought she was finally going to get to see her mother and Dickie, the fact of it was almost overwhelming. With tears glistening in her eyes, she asked, "What about Dickie?"

Her father's smile didn't quite reach his eyes as he replied, "You can see him now, and I'll just have to wait until your mother is ready to let me see him." Observing his sad eyes, she felt a twinge of guilt at her happiness, but she had waited too long for this moment to let it interfere with her own plans.

Bolting down her food, she hurried to her room to write the letter. Writing normally came easy to her, but this time as she stared at the blank sheet of paper, no words would come. About to get what she had dreamed about for years, she suddenly found herself worried. Had she changed so much that her mother might not know her? Would she recognize her mother and brother?

Moving to her vanity, she stared at her reflection in the mirror and took stock of the changes almost three years had brought. When she last saw her mother, she had just celebrated her eleventh birthday. Now almost fourteen years old, she no longer looked like the little girl her mother had left behind.

Thinking that all these questions soon would be answered, she returned to the task at hand, and in a few minutes had completed the letter. Addressed and stamped, it was ready to be mailed. She and Rose would walk downtown to the post office in the morning. Her last thought before falling asleep was to wonder what the response would be. In her dreams that night her mother dropped everything and flew to her side the moment she received the letter.

In actuality, when Priscilla read her daughter's letter in the familiar back slanted handwriting, she was, at first, undecided as to what she should do. Torn between her fear of losing Dickie and her desire to see her other two children, she had suppressed her inclination to rush to them.

Now, according to June's letter, Burrel wasn't demanding to see Dickie as a condition of this visit. Fortunately, although she had been putting in many overtime hours at the defense plant, she was going to be off this coming weekend. Tucking the letter into her purse, and heading for the kitchen to start dinner, she was already making plans for the trip.

She was worried about how Bill would react when he found out she would be going to Newark this weekend without him. Since their marriage they had spent all their free time together, but surely he would understand that it would be better the first time she saw the children if only she and Dickie went.

That night she sat in front of her dressing table, as June had done a few nights earlier, studying her reflection in the mirror, wondering if the children would think she'd changed. Other than her more fashionable hair style and well made up face, she could see no difference in her appearance. With the children, though, it was a different matter. From the pictures she carried in her mind and recent ones she carried in her wallet, she knew they had grown and changed.

Coming into the room, standing behind her and watching her face in the mirror, Bill asked, "Why so serious?" In response she handed June's letter to him. Opening and reading it, he asked, "When are you going?"

"I thought Dickie and I would go this Saturday," she responded. The omission of his name did not escape him, but contrary to what Priscilla feared, he did understand. He hadn't seen any of his children since he'd left West Virginia. He especially missed his son, little Bill, and he was aware if there ever came a time he would be allowed to see him, he wouldn't want to include Priscilla or Dickie in their first meeting. Reflecting on the bitterness his former wife and children felt toward him, he thought this wasn't something he'd have to face anytime soon.

He and Priscilla had never been comfortable talking to each other about their children. Early in their marriage, Priscilla had made it clear that Dickie was her son, and she would be responsible for raising him. If she felt that way about the one who lived with them, she would most certainly feel more strongly about the other two.

"You're so quiet," Priscilla said. "Are you upset?" His response of, "No," reassured her and she continued to talk, "I would like to go on Saturday. If Dickie and I leave before lunch, we should be able to be home before dark." Rustling through her purse she pulled out her ration book and said, "Since we've been riding the bus to work, I have enough gasoline rationing stamps to get there and back without any problems."

Sounding skeptical, he said, "Are you sure you'll be alright driving that far by yourself?" In response, she tilted her head back and laughed. "Good heavens, Bill, it's only fifty-five miles. Don't forget, I was driving in and around Newark years before I knew you existed."

The subtle change in his expression made her aware of her poor choice of words. She always tried to be careful not to remind him of her years with Burrel. To distract him, she hurried on to one of his favorite subjects. "The car looks great. Did you have it washed today?"

This question drew several comments about the car, along with an admonition to watch out for other drivers and to be careful where she parked it. Knowing how particular he was with all his possessions, she couldn't help wonder, "Is it me or the car, he's worrying about."

~

The next day she mailed a letter to June telling her that she and Dickie would be there early in the afternoon. Every day June had been meeting the mailman on the porch before he even had a chance to get to the mailbox. Handing her a stack of mail he grinned as he said, "I think the one on top is the one you've been waiting for."

Barely containing her excitement, she thanked him and waited patiently while he commented on the nice weather they were having. Once he turned to walk down the steps, she tore open the letter and read every word before going in the house.

"Was that the mailman?" Polly called from the kitchen. June handed the rest of the mail to her and sat at the table rereading her letter. Noticing her enthralled expression, Polly asked, "What do you have there?"

"A letter from Mom," she replied. "She and Dickie will be here Saturday afternoon. That's three whole days. I can hardly wait."

"The time will pass before you know it," Polly replied. "To help it go a little faster, you can just help me clean the house. I certainly don't want Priscilla to think I'm not a good housekeeper," she added.

"Mom," she groaned. "The house looks fine. You always keep it looking nice," she continued, as she looked around at the shiny floors and countertops. Polly's flurry of activity as she set out cleaning supplies made it obvious she wasn't going to be swayed. Knowing it was useless to argue, June resignedly asked, "What do you want me to do?"

Cecil walked in during this swirl of activity and soon found himself on a ladder, washing windows. "Just make them shine," Polly instructed, "Your mother and brother will be here Saturday, and I don't want them to think we live in a pig pen."

June and Cecil exchanged glances, but experience had taught them that it wouldn't do any good to object. "When are they coming?" he asked June. In response, she showed him the letter and they talked for a few minutes about the reality of finally seeing their mother and little brother until Polly called June inside to polish the furniture.

As Polly had predicted, the time appeared to go faster while they kept busy with their early fall house cleaning. If June even looked like she might be having a hard time waiting for Saturday, Polly found some other work to keep her occupied. "If I'd known Mom's visit meant we were going to have to do all this work, I wouldn't have said a word to her about it," she told Rose.

Saturday morning, June paced through the immaculate rooms, looking at her watch every five minutes. "Why don't you sit down?" Polly fumed. "Your mother said she'd be here in the afternoon. It's only ten o'clock now. You're going to drive me crazy before they get here."

June envied Cecil, still sleeping soundly. She knew he hadn't gotten much sleep the night before. While she'd been tossing and turning, too excited to fall asleep, she'd heard him climb through his window hours after midnight. He didn't seem as excited as she was about the upcoming visit. Although he'd never said, June suspected he still harbored some anger toward their mother for leaving him.

Her thoughts were interrupted by Polly's voice asking, "Isn't today the day Mace and Mabel are going to their church picnic at Moundbuilder's Park? Didn't you plan to go with Rose?" In response to her affirmative nod, Polly added, "I think you and Cecil should go ahead and go with them."

June turned with a startled expression and exclaimed, "Go to the picnic! Are you kidding? Mom and Dickie will be here sometime this afternoon. I'm certainly not going to miss them."

"I don't expect you to miss them, but I think you're going to blow a gasket if you just stay here waiting. If you don't, you're going to cause me to! You can go with Rose, and when your mother gets here I'll send her out to Moundbuilder's Park. I imagine she knows where it is."

"I'm sure she does," June said, remembering Aunt Mabel's story. The more she thought about it, the more the idea of meeting them at Moundbuilder's appealed to her. That way, they could be alone. This would solve one of the problems she'd been worrying about, having her two mothers together.

"I'll go tell Rose," she called out, as she dashed out the door. Returning a few minutes later, she told Polly, "We'll be leaving in twenty minutes. Tell Mom I'll either be at one of the picnic shelters or on the mounds. I'll be watching for her."

She was glad Polly had talked her into going. It was a more enjoyable way to make the time go by than cleaning the house. The church women were good cooks, and she and Rose quickly piled their plates high and found a place under a tree where they could sit and talk while they ate.

Afterwards, they took a walk around the mounds, but before they started, June let Aunt Mabel, Inez, and Annamae know where she would be so they could tell her mother if she got there before they got back.

This park was formerly burial and ceremonial ground for Hopewell Indians, who had made this their home centuries before. A large mound, shaped like an eagle with its wings widespread was in the center of the great circle mound. A wooden foot bridge crossed the gully separating the two mounds.

June and Rose had walked around the great circle mound and now stood leaning against the bridge railing, watching the activities around the grounds. Picnickers filled the shelter houses. Young couples were strolling, hand in hand, toward the mounds; others were sitting under the shade trees. A ball game was in progress, but none of this held June's interest.

~

As her eyes roved from one scene to another, she noticed a tall woman and boy walking toward them. She watched the sunlight touch the woman's short curly hair, bringing out its golden highlights. The long legged boy strolling along beside her had the same dark blonde hair, only his was a shade lighter. Better dressed than the average person here, the woman was wearing a blue dress of some silky material, silk hose and high heeled shoes, and the boy was in dark dress pants and a white shirt.

Still too far away for her to clearly make out their features, she continued to watch their progress toward the mounds. As they drew nearer, June found herself enveloped in a feeling of happiness when she realized those two people were her mother and brother. Now that the moment she had been waiting for had finally arrived, she felt suddenly shy. "It's Mom and Dickie," she whispered to Rose.

"So it is," Rose replied. "What are you waiting for? After waiting for three years, aren't you even going to say hello?" Young as she was, Rose didn't put up with much nonsense. "Go on, or I will!" she said.

The prospect of Rose greeting them before she did galvanized her into action. Walking down the steps, then running the last few yards, she called out, "Mom, Dickie!" as she threw herself into her mother's outstretched arms. Their laughter and tears mingled, as they hugged and kissed each other.

She felt as if all her senses were engulfed in a flood of sensations. The scent of her mother's familiar perfume, the softness and comfort of her mother's arms, the sound of her mother's voice, the sight of her mother's blue eyes brimming with tears, and her mother's happy smile brought back a flood of memories. It was like entering a time machine and being transported back in time to her early childhood, to the days when they lived in the cavern house or in Petersburg.

The hard core of pain and emptiness she'd been carrying inside her very being seemed to melt away, leaving her with a feeling of peace and happiness. The missing pieces had been replaced.

Dickie had been standing impatiently, watching the reunion. Turning her attention to him, she cried, "You've grown so tall. I've been thinking of you the way you were the last time I saw you. I guess I won't be able to call you my baby brother anymore."

Dickie grinned and said, "That's okay. I never did like that baby brother stuff, much." They stood looking at each other, smiling, trying to relate this grown up person to the child they'd known. "Maybe his legs are longer and his hair is darker, but he's still Dickie," June thought as she put her arm around him and gave him a big hug. "I've missed you," she whispered.

"Me too!" he responded. "It's good to have a brother and sister again." He eagerly looked around the park before he asked, "Where is Cecil?"

June no sooner started to tell him that he was somewhere in the park, when Dickie spotted Cecil and Inez walking down the steps from the mounds. His eyes lit up and he started to wave wildly, as he yelled, "Hey, Cecil! Cecil, we're over here!"

While Dickie continued to wave and call his name, Cecil ambled over to where they were standing, nonchalantly trying to act as if this were an everyday occurrence. Hard as he tried though, he wasn't able to maintain his cool, as he got closer and found himself almost smothered in a big bear hug as his little brother wrapped his arms around him and pounded him on the back while repeating his name over and over again. "Dad's wife said you were here, but I was beginning to wonder if you really were," Dickie said.

"Oh, you met Mom?" June inquired. "What did you think of her?" She might not have noticed the slight tightening of Priscilla's lips, if she weren't so attuned to her senses today. She made a mental note, never in front of her mother, to refer to Polly as "Mom".

"She has pretty hair," Priscilla replied. "I told her I would bring you home, but first, let's go have some ice cream. You'd better let your Aunt Mabel know I'll be taking you home," she instructed June.

After leaving the park, they went downtown to the soda fountain at Gallagher's Drug Store on the square where Cecil, June, and Dickie had banana splits while Priscilla sipped an ice cream soda. Despite the waitress's disapproving glances they sat for hours, trying to catch up on what had happened in all their lives. June felt that life couldn't be much better than this; being with her mother and brothers, in this town she loved, and living close enough to be able to see them often. "I'm so glad Dad didn't make us wait until Mom lets him see Dickie," she thought.

She hadn't imagined it possible anything could intrude upon her happiness today, but the thought of her dad's sad eyes when he'd talked about having to wait to see Dickie caused her to feel a momentary flicker of guilt. It didn't seem right to be this happy when her dad was still suffering from the pain of the separation from his son.

"What's wrong, June?" her mother asked. Not wanting to dampen their happy mood, June decided this wasn't the time, and she probably wasn't the person to talk about it. Help, in this matter, though, was to come from a surprising quarter before the day was over.

Finally, Priscilla looked at her watch and reluctantly exclaimed, "I don't want to break this up, but I think we're going to have to leave. I told Bill we'd be home before dark." Noticing June's look of disappointment, she tried to add a touch of levity by saying, "Besides, if we stay much longer, they're going to charge us rent." They smiled as they walked out into the late afternoon sunshine and around the square to where Priscilla had parked the car.

～

As she drove through the familiar streets of her hometown, Priscilla asked June and Cecil, "Would you like to come to Mansfield and spend a week with us before school starts?"

While Cecil nodded, June exclaimed, "I'd love it! But we'd have to ask M..." Remembering her mother's reaction the other time she'd called Polly "Mom", she quickly corrected herself to say she'd have to ask Polly.

"I'll go in with you and talk to her," Priscilla said. "I've been working a lot of overtime, but I think I'll be off next weekend and could come and get you."

June was filled with excitement at the prospect of spending an entire week with her mother and Dickie. "Surely she'll let us go," she thought, as they trooped across the porch to the front door. "We're back," she called to Polly as she led them into the wide entrance hall.

Entering from the kitchen, Polly smiled and said, "I just made some iced tea and have some cookies. If you'll make yourself at home in the living room I'll bring them in."

Settling into one of the cushioned chairs, idly trailing her fingers across the smooth shining maple surface of its wide arms, Priscilla studied her surroundings. "This is nice," she said. "Polly is a good housekeeper." Although she agreed, June could hardly contain the giggle that was bubbling up inside her, as she remembered the frenzy of housekeeping that had taken place during the few days prior to this visit.

While they were having their refreshments, the women engaged in small talk about the weather and the inconvenience of dealing with ration stamps. Placing her glass on the coffee table, Priscilla hesitantly broached the subject of June and Cecil's proposed visit. Polly listened politely until Priscilla had finished speaking before turning to Cecil and saying, "Why don't you take Dickie out to the garage and show him your car?" As the boys started to leave the room, prepared to stay and find out what Polly had to say, June was not happy to be told to go with the boys.

As she slowly walked past the open window, she overheard Polly say, "Did I understand you to say you wanted June and Cecil to visit you in a week or so? I think there is something else we need to talk about." Although tempted to stand by the window and listen, she decided against it. She didn't want to do anything to jeopardize her chance to visit their mother, so she hurriedly joined her brothers in the garage.

As she stepped through the doorway Dickie was saying, "Wow! I can't believe you're putting this car together yourself!"

"I'm not doing it all by myself," Cecil explained. "My friends Phil Haas and Johnny Bracken are helping me." Although Cecil would never have admitted it, he was enjoying the admiration of his younger brother as he followed him around the garage and listened to him explain what the car had looked like when they first got it, and all the things they'd done to get it to the point of almost being recognizable as an automobile.

June was only half listening to their conversation, as her thoughts were with the two women in the living room. "What in the world do they have to talk about for this long?" she wondered. "It shouldn't have taken that long for Mom to have said we could go." The more she thought about it, the more convinced she became that it wasn't going to happen.

If she had continued to eavesdrop outside the open window she would have been as startled to hear Polly's next comments as Priscilla had been. "Don't you think, if Burrel and I consider letting June and Cecil see you, you should let Burrel see Dickie?"

Alarmed Priscilla leapt to her feet and cried out, "I can't do that!" Standing, as if poised for flight, her blue eyes blazing and her jaw firm, she confronted Polly with, "I don't know how much you know about this, but when the divorce came through, Burrel wrote that he'd been awarded custody of Dickie. He said he expected me to turn him over to him. You can tell him, I'm not giving Dickie up."

"Sit down, Priscilla. Let me get us some coffee, and let's talk," Polly said. "I didn't mean to frighten you. When you get to know me a little better you'll find out, I say what I think." Listening to her speak, Priscilla's tension gradually eased and she returned to her chair.

"I'll just be a minute," Polly said as she hurried to the kitchen, returning seconds later with two cups of steaming coffee. Settling on the couch across from where Priscilla was seated, her voice sounded firm when she continued speaking. "Burrel was angry and hurt when he wrote that letter. He might have meant it when he wrote it, but I can guarantee you that if you let Dickie come here, he'll be coming back to you at the end of the visit."

Priscilla had been studying Polly's face and listening intently to everything she said. Though every word sounded sincere, Priscilla felt compelled to ask, "How can you guarantee something like that?"

"I'll tell you what I told Burrel months ago," Polly replied, "I have my hands full raising his other two. I have no intention of raising another one. I can assure you he's not going to take Dickie because as his wife I'd never agree to it. It would be different if Dickie needed to live with us; I'd take him in a minute. Since he's got a mama who wants him, he needs to stay where he is. I've already told Burrel what I'm telling you. He knows I mean what I'm saying, and you'd better believe it too."

A little unnerved by this blunt outspoken woman, Priscilla sat quietly for a moment as she mulled over what she'd just heard. Finally breaking the silence, she replied, "I don't want to come across as vindictive. It's just that I don't want to lose Dickie. I need some time to think about this before I make a decision." She paused for a second before adding, "You certainly have given me some food for thought."

Polly nodded, then declared, "Before you leave, let me ask you what you think Bill would say if you told him you were going to bring June and Cecil home for him to raise." Priscilla's eyes widened in alarm at the prospect of delivering that news to her husband. Her change of expression wasn't lost on Polly, who laughed as she said, "That's the way I feel about raising another child. Now don't get me wrong, I'm sure Dickie is a nice little boy and since he's Burrel's son, I would love him as much as I do June and Cecil. But you never have to worry, he's yours and as long as you want him, we would never take him away from you."

"I can see what you mean," Priscilla said. "For the first time since the divorce, I feel safe letting Dickie see his father. If I come for June and Cecil next weekend, Dickie can stay here for a couple hours and visit with Burrel. I can go over to my brother Fred's while he's here, then stop by for all three of the children when it's time to go home. We can do the same thing when I bring June and Cecil back the next weekend."

Although Polly had been nodding her agreement as Priscilla was talking, she thought it might be wiser to talk to Burrel before she gave Priscilla a definite answer. Voicing this concern she said, "I think that sounds fine, but I'd better run that by Burrel first. I'm pretty sure he'll agree, but he is going to want to know when Dickie can come and spend a week or two with us."

Priscilla only hesitated a moment before responding, "By the time June and Cecil's visit is over, it's going to be time for school to start. I'll promise to let him come for a couple weeks next summer if Burrel will go along with that."

Her eyes and smile were reassuring as Polly replied, "Don't worry. Burrel will be happy to hear that he's going to get to see Dickie. I'm pretty sure he'll agree." Nodding toward the sound of the voices of the reunited siblings as they talked outside the open window, she added, "I imagine they're getting anxious to know what we've been talking about. Shall we go out and tell them?"

Priscilla nodded, then glanced at her watch before exclaiming, "Good heavens! I had no idea it was so late. I told Bill I'd be home before dark. Even if I left this minute, I wouldn't be able to make it."

When June, Dickie, and Cecil heard Priscilla and Polly come out onto the porch, they strolled over to the steps and looked up at them expectantly. Not waiting to be asked, Polly told them, "We're trying to work things out so you'll be able to spend some time together. We'll know more after I've had a chance to talk to your dad."

They all felt so confident Burrel would agree to let them go, that their farewell hugs and kisses were mingled with cries of, "See you next week." As Priscilla drove away, June and Cecil stood on the sidewalk in front of their house, watching and waving. They could see and hear Dickie with his head poked out the front window, waving and yelling, "Goodbye, June! Goodbye, Cecil! See you next week," until the car disappeared from their sight.

Their mother's car had barely turned the corner when they saw their dad's familiar tan and brown Chevrolet approaching. Stepping out of the car, he asked, "Did your mom and Dickie come today?"

"They haven't been gone a minute," Cecil said. "If you came up Everett Avenue, you probably passed them." Watching him as he replied that he couldn't have seen them since he'd taken the other route today, June wasn't surprised to see a momentary look of pain flicker across his face.

As they all trooped onto the porch and into the house, he asked, "Well, how was your visit? Did you all have a good time?"

Then, not waiting for a reply, he blurted out what had been on his mind all day, "How does Dickie look? Has he grown?" Then, hesitantly, as if fearful of their response, he added, "Did he ask about me?" When June was able to tell him Dickie had indeed inquired about him, his face lit up like a kid at Christmas.

After hearing the news about seeing Dickie next week, being a quiet man, it wasn't in his nature to express his pleasure the way a more boisterous man might, but within his heart there were shouts of glee and sounds of happiness. "What in the world did you say to Priscilla to get her to change her mind?" he asked Polly.

In response, she just smiled and said, "Oh, you know how it is when women get together, just a little woman talk." Laughing at his puzzled expression, she continued, "I forgot to tell you, she would like to have June and Cecil spend a week or so with her. I told her I thought it would be alright, but I needed to ask you."

As he listened, a frown creased his brow as he said, "Now let me get this straight, she wants June and Cecil for a week or two, and I get to see Dickie for a couple hours. That doesn't sound right to me. What gives?"

Polly reminded him that school would be starting soon, and there just wasn't time for Dickie to come this summer. "Priscilla did promise she'd let him come next summer for a couple weeks. We've made some progress today. Let's not do anything to destroy it," she said.

Being able to see the wisdom of what she was saying, he conceded. "You're right. I don't know how you accomplished it, but it looks to me as if you worked a miracle. I was beginning to think, I was going to have to wait until Dickie grew up before I got to see him." Planting a kiss on her upturned face, he said "Thanks, Honey."

"I was wondering how you two would get along. Was meeting her difficult for you?" he asked. His comment seemed to startle her. She remained quiet for a few seconds as if she were trying to collect her thoughts.

"No. I don't have any reason not to like Priscilla. After all, she is June and Cecil's mother. She must have done something right when she was raising them, or they wouldn't have turned out as well as they have," she said. In response to his skeptical look, she added, "Besides, if she hadn't left when she did, we wouldn't be here together. Furthermore, I know it would be better for the kids if we could all get along."

He nodded, but his emotions were in turmoil at the thought of all three of his children in Priscilla and Bill's home. He couldn't imagine ever feeling toward Bill the way Polly did toward Priscilla. Knowing that Bill had pursued and courted Priscilla back in West Virginia when Burrel was working out of state to make a living for his family angered him. He still blamed Bill for the break-up of his family. Burrel didn't intend to ever have to see him and certainly not voluntarily.

No matter what emotions the parents might be feeling, for the next week June's mood swung from anticipation at the prospect of spending that much time with her mother and Dickie to a sense of apprehension at the thought of seeing Bill in his new position as her stepfather.

Fortunately, in this final week of her baby-sitting job, Butch and Beth had kept her so busy that the time seemed to fly. Aware she would be leaving them; they never left her side for a minute. This was fine with her as she had become very fond of her young charges and saw to it this week was a memorable one. After days filled with their favorite activities, Saturday morning found the two children standing on the porch with their parents waving as June and her father rode away. June watched this scene in the rear view mirror until the distance separated them from her view. Sighing softly, she murmured, "I'm going to miss those two."

"I know you will," Burrel replied. Then changing the subject, he said, "Your mother will be here in a little over an hour. That will give you time to get your clothes packed before they arrive." Smiling happily, June nodded, then leaning her head back against the car seat she closed her eyes, and spent the rest of the trip home, daydreaming about the upcoming reunion. Since her dad also seemed to be lost in thoughts of his own, they rode the rest of the way in companionable silence.

∼

After they got home, June hurriedly got ready, then positioned herself on the front porch, watching for her mother's car. When she saw it turn the corner onto Lawrence Street, she ran inside shouting, "They're here! They're here!"

"Don't keep them waiting," Burrel said. "Go on outside to meet them." In response to her urging him to come too, he resisted, "I'll wait until your mother leaves." A persistent knocking interrupted their conversation and sent June scurrying to answer it.

Through the screen door she could see her mother standing as if poised for flight. Dickie, in his best Sunday clothes, was impatiently waiting beside her. After they'd exchanged hugs, Priscilla told them she'd be back for them in a couple hours. As June walked to the car with her mother, the term "Beat a hasty retreat" popped into her mind. She wondered if the day would ever come when her parents would want to be in the same room. It certainly didn't look very promising.

She was so absorbed watching her mother drive away that she almost missed the reunion between her dad and Dickie. Turning just in time, she saw her dad open the door and heard him softly say, "Hello, Son." Both of these two important males in her life stood looking at each other, grinning. Then Burrel held out his hand and took Dickie's in his, almost formally shaking it.

Dickie looked into his dad's smiling eyes and said, "Hi, Dad. It's good to see you!" No sooner had the words left his mouth, then he found himself engulfed in a big bear hug. Watching this scene, June thought she saw a tear escape from her dad's eye. She decided she must have imagined it, though, because when he released his youngest son, he was smiling.

They spent the next couple hours talking, laughing, and visiting while June and Polly saw to it the lemonade glasses and the cookie plate never had a chance to become empty. Dickie told them how much he liked sports, and how he wanted to get on the football and basketball teams when he was older.

He regaled them with tales of his encounters with his older competitor while selling newspapers. His father sat back, quietly smiling and proudly listening as his younger son talked. "I'm looking forward to next summer when you'll get to spend more time with us," Burrel said. Dickie said that he too was looking forward to it.

In the course of the afternoon Mace, Mabel, and the girls came over to see him. As Burrel had earlier, they all commented on how much he had grown. In his father's mind, he had still been the tow headed eight year old boy he'd last seen so long ago.

The time passed much too quickly, and it was soon time for Priscilla to come for them. June and Cecil had already brought their bags downstairs and were ready to leave when they saw her park in front of the house. While they were stowing their luggage in the car, Burrel and Dickie said their farewells. Knowing they would be seeing each other the following weekend made the parting easier.

For the drive to Mansfield, June claimed the front seat next to her mother while the boys piled into the back. Rubbing her hand across the upholstery June commented, "This is a nice car. It looks new."

"It's not," Priscilla said. "But Bill is so particular and takes such good care of it that it looks as good as new." The mention of Bill reminded June that he would be there when they got to her mother's home in Mansfield. The thought raced across her mind of the many visits Bill had made to their home in West Virginia, under the pretense of visiting her mother's friend. She remembered the children at school teasing her about the bread man's truck being parked in front of their home so often. When Bill's bread truck had been broken into outside their house, and all the bread, muffins, and cakes strewn around the yard, the culprit had never been caught. June still secretly believed that her brother Cecil had vented his frustrations about Bill intruding on their family. She wondered what it would be like to see him again.

Although over the years this road leading to Mansfield would become very familiar to them, on this trip everything was new and unfamiliar. Passing through St. Louisville, their mother pointed out the store her father had owned while Cecil was a baby, but she didn't mention her life there with their father. If traveling through this little village brought back memories of her life with Burrel and Cecil, as a toddler, she kept it well hidden.

~

It was still daylight when she brought the car to a stop in front of their house. "We're here," she called, as much to Bill, who was coming down the walk to meet them, as to her three passengers.

After kissing Priscilla on the cheek, Bill said hello to June and Cecil and asked Dickie to help them take their bags to their rooms. A flurry of activity followed while they settled in. Finally, the time came when they had to go downstairs and face their new stepfather.

They hadn't known him very well when they'd lived in West Virginia. One thing she remembered was hearing that he was lively and full of fun and known in Petersburg as quite a lady's man. This quiet, sober man bore no resemblance to the man June remembered or had heard so much about.

"Have you eaten?" he asked. When Priscilla told him they hadn't, he turned to June and Cecil and said, "There's a little restaurant downtown where they have the best coney islands in town. I thought we'd go there." They found that even though the restaurant wasn't very fancy, the food was good. June and Cecil had no way of knowing whether these coney islands were the best in Mansfield, but they certainly were the best they'd ever tasted.

As several of the patrons stopped at their table to talk, it became obvious that Priscilla, Bill, and Dickie were well known here. June and Cecil didn't remember all the people they met that evening, but they did remember the good food and the good time they'd had.

The next day passed quickly as their Mansfield relatives came to see June and Cecil. After the aunts, uncles and cousins went home, Priscilla took June, Cecil, and Dickie for a ride and showed them around Mansfield.

The downtown area was built on many hills. Being Sunday, all the businesses were closed, but as they rode by they were able to see into the stores, catching a glimpse of the well-stocked racks. Like Newark, Mansfield boasted a downtown square, but unlike Newark, their main shopping area branched off from it.

Before returning to the house, Priscilla pointed out the defense plants where she and Bill worked and Mac's Diner, where she'd waited tables when she first came to Mansfield.

When they'd left, Bill had been tilted back in his chair, sound asleep. When they returned, it appeared he hadn't moved from that position. During their visit he was pleasant to them and made them feel welcome, but he never intruded on their time with Dickie and their mother.

That week, while the adults were at work, the young people were left to their own devices. Most days found them at the swimming pool where Dickie proudly introduced them to his friends. Days when they didn't go swimming, they'd walk downtown to a movie. This was a bittersweet time for all of them. It was great being together again, but underneath their cheerfulness was the awareness that they would never again be the same family. June and Cecil would be going home to their dad and Polly, while Dickie would be staying here with their mother and Bill. If June hadn't thought about it before, hearing Dickie call Bill "Dad" certainly brought it home to her.

"It's no different for him to do that then it is for us to call Polly 'Mom'," June thought. After all, he'd been living with Bill as his father longer than they'd been living with Polly as their mother.

In a prominent spot in the living room was a framed picture of a little boy of about Dickie's age. When she first saw it, June thought it was Dickie, but after a closer look she knew she was mistaken. Observing her studying the picture, Priscilla said, "That's Bill's son, Little Bill."

When June told her at first she'd thought it was Dickie, Priscilla replied, "I don't think they look alike, but they are the same age." Then, as if thinking aloud, she reflected, "Bill misses him. He hasn't seen him since he came out here."

June felt a pang of pity for this silent man. Thinking about how much she'd wanted to see her mother, June remarked, "Little Bill probably misses his dad as much as Bill misses him. Maybe some time they can get together."

"I seriously doubt it," Priscilla replied. "I don't think Bill's ex-wife will ever let him see little Bill." This sounded familiar to June, but she didn't voice her thoughts. She couldn't help think, though, that since things were working out for them, things were bound to work out for Bill.

As it turned out, Priscilla's prediction was correct. Although, the little boy's picture remained on display, even when he became a man, Bill never again saw his son.

～

This was not to be the end of June and Priscilla's serious conversation. Later that evening while Bill was napping in the living room, and the boys had gone to see one of Dickie's friends, they went for a walk around the neighborhood.

Strolling together like this reminded June of living in Petersburg and the two of them walking to Site's restaurant for a Pepsi. Engrossed in her memories, she was startled to hear her mother say, "I never meant to leave you and Cecil. When I left I intended to come back and get you."

Since this was a subject she hadn't expected they would be discussing, June found herself overwhelmed by emotion. She felt like screaming, "Why didn't you?" but instead she stood still, looking into her mother's eyes and waiting for her to continue.

By now, tears were filling Priscilla's eyes, as she said, "When I left, I was really naive. I thought I could come out here and get a job, find a place to rent and send for both of you. What happened, though, was that the job I found only paid ten dollars a week. Dickie and I had to live with my niece, Velma, and her husband since I couldn't even afford to pay for a sleeping room, let alone get a place big enough for all of us."

"You could have come back," June said. "I wrote and told you how much I missed you." As she looked into her daughter's questioning eyes, Priscilla despaired of ever making her understand.

"You'll never know how close I came to coming back when I got your letter asking me to come home, but I'd seen other people leave their husbands and go back to them, and I decided if I ever left, I'd never return."

Outwardly June appeared calm, but her thoughts were in turmoil as she reflected on how her mother's stubbornness had kept them from being reunited as a family.

"You were too young to understand, but your dad and I hadn't been happy for a long time. Things are better this way. Bill and I are happy together, and it didn't take your dad long to find someone else," Priscilla said.

Observing the slight tightening of her mother's lips when she uttered the last few words, June was surprised to realize that her mother appeared to feel jealous of Polly. Not for the first time, she thought, "I'll never understand this woman."

June had been too absorbed in their conversation to notice Cecil and Dickie's approach until they almost bumped into them. The boys were on their way to the soda fountain at the neighborhood drug store, and they invited them to join them.

Visibly relieved by the interruption, Priscilla treated them all to banana splits while she ordered coffee. The boys were full of high spirits that soon proved to be contagious. By the time they left the soda fountain, everyone was in a happy, relaxed frame of mind.

It was to be years before either mother or daughter returned to the topic of their interrupted conversation. This was fine with June. Happy being reunited with her mother, she preferred to dwell on that happiness, rather than dredge up the painful past. Before falling asleep she was struck by a thought that caused her to giggle. "I'm like Scarlet O'Hara. I'll think about it tomorrow."

~

As Priscilla had promised, she did let Dickie spend a couple more hours with his dad when she brought them home. Dropping the boys off at the house on Lawrence Street, she took June with her to see her brother Fred and his wife Lidy. As Mace and Mabel had, with Dickie, they commented on how much June had grown. When they'd last seen her, she'd been a little girl, and now she was almost as tall as her mother.

Aunt Lidy was disappointed, though, to learn that June had lost most of her accent. "You say pie just like everyone else," she said. "I always loved to hear you and your brothers say piah." Her aunt's comments pleased June, as one of her goals was to lose her accent. It appeared she was succeeding.

Saying goodbye to her mother and brother this time wasn't as difficult since they all knew they would be seeing each other soon. After the car disappeared from their view, they trudged back into the house. Almost immediately they had to turn their attention to getting ready for the start of a new school year.

CHAPTER SIXTEEN

LIFE WITH RATION STAMPS

The day after Labor Day, dressed in their new school clothes, June walked along with Rose for her first day at Lincoln Junior High, while Cecil and Inez headed in the opposite direction to Newark High School. Their homes on Lawrence Street were situated between the two schools.

Since Rose was in a lower grade, the two girls had to separate as soon as they entered the building. June was again dreading going into a strange classroom, but June Hickman, the girl who sat behind her in homeroom, took it upon herself to show her around and introduce her to the other students.

The two Junes were opposite in appearance. Less than five feet tall, June Hickman had naturally curly brown hair and brown eyes. She was so much smaller than all the other girls in the class, causing them to look at her as much younger than her actual age. June thought this was ridiculous. In her estimation, her new friend was one of the most mature girls in the school.

For the next four years, since they were in homeroom and most classes together, the two girls became a familiar sight as they walked to and from their classes. The difference in their height elicited some good-natured kidding from their classmates. Undaunted, they dubbed themselves "the long and the short of it all". In addition June developed her own circle of friends from school, but none could ever replace Rose as her best friend.

As it turned out, Cecil wasn't the only new student in his classes. A boy named Bill Cleaver had just moved to Newark from Wisconsin. The two boys found they shared more common interests than being strangers in a new school, and Bill became a familiar sight at the house on Lawrence Street.

The house was soon filled with the laughter of June and Cecil's friends. A favorite activity of the girls was making fudge. This innocent appearing pastime almost got June in trouble with her dad.

It was no secret in the family that Burrel felt he needed his cup of coffee to face the day. One morning, freshly shaven, but still rubbing the sleep from his eyes, he sat down at the breakfast table, picked up his coffee cup and took a long swig. Sputtering, he roared, "What in the world is wrong with this coffee?"

Feigning innocence, Polly replied with a question of her own. "What do you mean, what's wrong with the coffee? Mine tastes fine." She could say this in all honesty, but she knew what he was taking about. He liked his much sweeter than hers, almost syrupy sweet, and because of the previous night's fudge making, the sugar canister was almost empty. This wasn't the worst of it; they had used up the last of the month's sugar ration stamps.

A puzzled expression crossed his face, when she asked if he'd liked the fudge the girls had made the night before. "Sure it was good," he responded. "But what does that have to do with my coffee?"

"Think about it," she said. As realization hit, he let out a heartfelt moan. Polly had always been so good about monitoring their ration stamps; he'd never before had to give it a second thought. This episode with the fudge had changed that.

From now on, he informed Polly, fudge making was going to have to wait until after new ration stamps came out, and then the girls could only use whatever sugar was left over at the end of the month.

Grumbling, he finished his coffee, but for the first time since she'd known him, he left for work without having his second cup. His last words to Polly before he walked out the door were, "Don't forget to tell June." As he stomped off the porch, she could hear him mutter, "What's this world coming to? A man should be able to have sugar for his coffee."

Driving to work, though, his mood lightened when he reflected that he was lucky, if using all his sugar was the worse problem he had with his daughter. He had to remind himself of that thought every morning for the rest of the month until they received their new ration stamps.

~

This wasn't to be June's only encounter with ration stamps. Her fourteenth birthday was approaching, and her friends were planning a surprise birthday party for her. The abrupt way they'd stopped talking when she came into the room had given her a clue that something was going on. Like a kid pretending she still believed in Santa Claus, she didn't let them know she suspected.

She had already decided she was going to wear her new red and navy plaid pleated skirt and matching navy cardigan to the party. A few days before the big event, she stood before the mirror, modeling her new outfit. As she turned from side to side, surveying it from all angles, her brow became creased in a deep frown. Everything looked perfect until she looked at her feet. She'd never liked her brown shoes, but the last time she'd bought shoes Polly had told her that since they were rationed, she had to buy practical ones.

"Ugly! Ugly!" she grumbled as she stared at them. No matter how much polish she put on them, or how hard she tried to shine them, she couldn't make them look fashionable.

She knew the red penny loafers, she'd had her eyes on in the window of Nobel's Shoe Store on the square would be perfect for this outfit. She'd first seen them when she and Rose had gone downtown to see a movie and afterwards made their way around the square, stopping to look in every window along the way. Since then, every time she'd gone downtown she'd stopped and looked longingly at them. Although with shoes rationed, they weren't practical, she yearned to own them.

She had enough money saved from her summer job to buy a new pair. Polly had given her the ration stamp with instructions to buy a pair she could wear with everything. With this good advice ringing in her ears, she and Rose walked downtown to the shoe store.

All the words of advice and all thoughts of being practical disappeared when the clerk slipped the red loafers onto her feet. "They're perfect," she breathed, as she walked up and down the carpeted aisles.

Catching sight of herself in the full-length mirror settled it for her. She had to have these shoes. "I'll take them," she said before common sense had a chance to intervene.

Rose reassured her on the way home, reminding her that she had the right to get whatever shoes she wanted. Polly wasn't quite so understanding. "I can't believe you'd buy red shoes. Now just what do you have you can wear them with?" she demanded. "You've always been such a level headed girl! Whatever possessed you to do such a thing?"

Coming in on the end of the conversation, Burrel couldn't imagine what his daughter could have done to bring on her mother's wrath. "What's going on here?" he inquired. "What in the world has June done?"

Puzzled when Polly pointed to June's feet, he looked from his obviously upset wife to his unrepentant daughter, and said, "I still don't get it. Why don't you just tell me what she did?"

"Don't you see what she's wearing? She used her ration stamp to buy red shoes," Polly stormed. "She won't be able to buy anymore for months. That is the most impractical thing she's ever done."

A slow smile creased Burrel's face as he realized what she was talking about. "Is that all?" he asked. "I thought she'd done something really bad." Then in a more serious vein he sternly exclaimed, "Leave her alone! If she wants red shoes, she can have them."

First eyeing her daughter then her husband, she decided it was useless to argue. She might win against one of them, but she was no match when they joined forces.

"Alright", she announced. "If she made a mistake, she's just going to have to live with it."

When June's friends surprised her with the birthday party, she felt very stylish in her new red shoes. Over the next few months she proudly wore them, and never regretted her choice, despite her mother's dire prediction.

~

One day as June and Butch walked downtown to get a soda, he remarked, "June, you are different from other girls I know. I've never met anyone else who would use her one ration stamp to buy red shoes, but they really are hip." June smiled when she thought about the battles she'd had with her mother when she bought these shoes.

A few minutes later, after they sat down in a booth at their favorite ice cream fountain and ordered ice cream sodas, June could tell that Butch was antsy as if he had something to tell her. She wasn't prepared though when with a big grin he blurted out, "I joined the navy today!"

While she sat in stunned silence he asked, "What's the matter? Aren't you happy for me?"

"Sure I'm happy for you. I'm just surprised. I didn't think you would be enlisting until you were eighteen," she responded.

He explained that his dad had signed for him so he wouldn't have to wait until his birthday in October to join. She knew how he felt as she bemoaned the fact that she was still too young to join the WAVES, the women's branch of the navy. She shouldn't have been surprised at his news as most of the young men were patriotic and going into the service as soon as they were able.

Quickly, the time came for Butch to leave for basic training, then on to somewhere in the South Pacific. He wrote to June often and she was a dedicated letter writer, sending the letters to The Fleet Post Office in San Francisco. Trying to protect any military secrets, the censors cut out any words they thought might reveal too much. One night June moaned to Polly, "Mom, it's such a challenge trying to read Butch's letters the way the censors chop them up."

She held the letter she had received up so her mom could see the holes in it. "This letter I got from him today says "Dear June, today we..." she said as she made a scissors cutting motion to indicate that the next few words had been cut out. Then laughingly she went through the rest of the letter with only an occasional word remaining before she added, "Love, Butch."

Polly laughed and replied, "I can see how that can be frustrating."

CHAPTER SEVENTEEN

A NARROW ESCAPE

Her displeasure with June about the red shoe incident was soon forgotten when she found herself faced with the prospect of Cecil becoming a very young, very reluctant bridegroom.

The events leading up to his dilemma had started innocently enough the previous week. Saturday night June, Burrel, and Polly had been sitting in the living room while Cecil was upstairs in his room. June, as usual, had her nose stuck in a book while the adults were listening to the radio.

Lifting her head, June sniffed the air. The scent of Old Spice after-shave filled her nostrils. "Cecil must have a date tonight," she said, seconds before the object of her comment sauntered into the room.

"Wow!" she exclaimed as she looked up at him. Freshly shaven, every hair in place, he was wearing the new sweater and trousers he'd gotten for his birthday. "You're certainly all dolled up, who are you going out with?" she asked.

As he checked his reflection in the mirror, he ran a comb through his hair, all the while trying to ignore her. She was persistent though, "You don't really think a hair could escape, with all that gook you have on it?" she teased, before continuing her probing. "What did you say her name is?"

"I didn't say," he responded. "You don't know her anyway. Herb and I are going skating in Zanesville with a couple girls."

164

"You're going all the way to Zanesville!" Polly exclaimed. "What time are you going to be home?"

This brought an anguished response from Cecil, "Aw, Mom, I'm sixteen years old. When are you going to stop treating me like a kid?"

Burrel, who had been sitting quietly listening to this interchange, interjected, "He's right. He is growing up. I wasn't much older than he is when I was working in the wheat fields in North Dakota."

"You're a big help," Polly said before again turning her attention to Cecil. "Just don't be out too late and be careful driving to Zanesville."

The sound of Herb's footsteps on the porch gave him an excuse to escape from his sister's teasing and Polly's motherly advice. "Gotta go, Mom," he called over his shoulder as he bounded out the door to join his friend.

Everything was fine on the drive to Zanesville, and even better when they got to the skating rink. Both girls were vivacious. Cecil's date, Jane, was a petite blue-eyed blonde, while Herb's date, Evelyn, was a tall willowy brunette.

Holding hands with their dates, they skated to the swing music blaring from the speakers scattered throughout the large cavernous room. They hadn't realized how quickly the time had passed until Jane caught a glimpse of the wall clock, as they whirled by, and exclaimed, "I didn't know it was so late! Mom said I had to be home by midnight."

They hurriedly turned in their shoe skates and headed for the car. As Herb and Evelyn settled into the back seat and Jane snuggled close to Cecil in front, he asked, "Do you think we have time to stop for a hamburger and coke?"

Checking her watch, Jane responded, "Maybe we can get a coke to take with us, but we don't have time to go into the restaurant. If I'm out past midnight one more time, I'll be in real trouble."

Cecil stopped at the nearest gas station, and he and Herb went inside, returning with cold soft drinks. As he handed Jane's to her he said, "We have almost an hour. You'll be safely home in plenty of time."

As the miles whipped by under the wheels of his nineteen thirty-two Chevrolet, its occupants were in a jovial mood, talking, laughing and enjoying having the highway all to themselves. Herb bragged to the girls, "Did you know that Cecil and Phil reassembled a Austin car that was all in pieces?"

Impressed, Jane said, "Wow, Cecil, is that true?"

"Yeah, I used the money I got from selling the Austin, plus more I made from working at the railroad yard, to buy this Chevrolet," Cecil responded. A loud "bang" and a wild veering of the vehicle put an end to their frivolity. As the girls screamed, Cecil found himself fighting to keep the car from going over an embankment. Clutching his arm, Jane cried, "What's going on?"

Muttering under his breath, he managed to free himself from her grip and bring the car to a stop. Opening the door, he stepped out onto the berm and stood surveying the damage. "It's a flat!" he exclaimed as he stood staring at the left front tire. Herb, Jane and Evelyn walked up beside him and confirmed his diagnosis.

Rolling up his shirtsleeves and heading for the trunk, Herb said, "You do have a spare and a jack, don't you?" Cecil didn't immediately respond, but his glum expression caused Herb to cry out in alarm, "You don't, do you?"

"Oh, yes. I have a jack and a spare, but I'm not sure it will do us any good with these tires," Cecil replied. For the first time, he was sorry he'd traded the Austin for this car. Sure he'd had trouble with the timing on it, but that car didn't have the problem this one did.

Before he'd bought this Chevrolet, the previous owner had told him there was something unusual about the way the wheel was constructed that made it necessary to break it down before the tire could be removed. With the confidence of youth, Cecil hadn't considered it important at the time. Now, one half hour before midnight, on this deserted highway halfway between Newark and Zanesville, with a date who had trusted him to get her home on time, he fervently wished he'd taken it more seriously.

Though he felt it was useless, he and Herb set about jacking up the car and trying to remove the tire. Jane and Evelyn looked on, keeping up a steady stream of encouraging words.

"No one is going to believe that old excuse about having a flat tire," Cecil said. Herb laughed, and the girls nervously giggled. "I hate to tell you this," Cecil said. "It's going to take a mechanic to get this tire off. Unless someone comes along, who can give us a ride into town, we're going to be out all night."

They all expressed concern about what their parents would say, but decided to make the best of it. "There's bound to be a car coming along soon." Jane said. "If so, Evelyn and I can get it to stop. We'll do what Claudette Colbert did in It Happened One Night." In case anyone had missed the movie, she demonstrated by lifting her skirt a few inches above her knee while jauntily waving her thumb in the air.

The boys showed their appreciation with loud piercing wolf whistles. "I bet, in real life someone would have stopped for Clark Gable just as fast," Herb exclaimed.

"I would have," the girls cried in unison. "I really liked him in Gone With The Wind," Evelyn said. This light banter continued while they scanned the distance for the sight of automobile lights.

After about an hour of watching and waiting, the chill of the night air forced them back into the car. They talked for awhile and engaged in some light necking before finally falling asleep.

After being awakened by the morning sun shining through the windows, Cecil glanced at his watch and muttered, "It's almost seven o'clock." His voice didn't quite hide the apprehension he was feeling. He didn't know the girls' parents, but he did know his and Herb's and shuddered to think what they must be going through. The worry and concern must be as bad, or even worse, in the girls' homes.

His gloomy thoughts were interrupted by the sound of an approaching vehicle. As it drew nearer, he and his companions jumped out of the car and stood waving their arms and yelling, "Stop!"

No sooner had Jane cried, "He's going on!" than the driver screeched to a stop a few feet beyond where they were standing. A woman, who looked to be about Polly's age, stuck her head out the passenger's window and asked, "What's the problem? What are you doing out here this time of morning?"

After they'd explained their dilemma, Cecil said, "We need a ride into town. If you'd drop us off at a gas station, I could call my dad, and he could come and pick us up."

"We're not going into town," the woman explained. "We're going to my parents' house. It's just down the road a few miles. If you give us your father's phone number, I'll call and tell him where you are."

Before Cecil could reply, Jane said, "I'll give you mine so you can call my mother, too. She's really going to be upset."

The woman shook her head as she said, "We'll make the call to this young man's father. If you give me the other numbers, I'll pass them on to him. I'm sure he'll let your parents know what's happened."

"I'm sure Mom will," Cecil said as the girls searched their purses and the boys their pockets and the car's glove compartment for paper and pencil. Cecil found an envelope and a stub of a pencil. Jane hurriedly wrote all their names and phone numbers, underlining Cecil's.

Tucking the paper into her purse, the woman assured them she'd deliver the messages as soon as they reached their destination. Before leaving, the male driver, who'd been silent until this point, apologized. "I feel bad about leaving you kids out here like this. I'd take you home, but with our kids asleep in the back seat, there wouldn't be room. I'm sure your dad could be here by the time I took them to their grandparents and came back for you." After Cecil and his friends assured them they'd be fine and expressed their appreciation for what they were going to do for them, the Good Samaritans continued on their journey.

"It shouldn't be too long now," Herb said. The rumbling in his stomach caused him to add, "I could certainly use something to eat, about now."

"I've got a couple candy bars," Evelyn said. "We can share them." While this meager fare didn't compare with the bacon and eggs they'd be eating if they were safely at home, it helped calm the gnawing pangs in their stomachs.

When Polly heard the strange woman's voice on the phone, her already mounting alarm increased. "What is it? What's happened to Cecil?"

The woman quickly reassured her and delivered the messages. After being sure she had all the information she needed, she fervidly thanked the caller and proceeded to relay Cecil's message to Burrel.

Visibly relieved, Burrel patted her on the shoulder, planted a kiss on her forehead and cheerfully said, "I told you he was alright. You've been worrying for nothing."

"For nothing!" she exploded. "He was out all night! For all I knew, he could have been lying dead somewhere."

"Be thankful he's alright," he told her, then continued soothingly to add, "I was worried, too. I guess I'd better get a move on. They've been out there long enough."

He was no sooner out the door, than she sat down by the phone and started to call Herb, Jane, and Evelyn's parents. Herb's and Evelyn's mothers were gracious and appreciative, but Jane's mother was another matter. No sooner did she hear Polly say they'd had a flat tire, than she started screaming in Polly's ear, "You expect me to believe that! You know as well as I do what they were up to!" She continued in this vein for what seemed an eternity. With the little sleep Polly had the night before, she was in no mood to listen to this stranger's hysterical raving.

Then realizing the woman had probably been as worried as she had been, she swallowed her angry retort and instead responded in a placating tone, "Thank God, the children are safe. That's all that matters now."

"That's alright for you to say! Don't think for a minute this is the end of it," she yelled, before slamming the receiver in Polly's ear. Standing, holding the dead phone in her hand, Polly mused, "She sure is a strange one."

Burrel had been confidant he could change the tire, but he was no more successful than the boys had been. Admitting defeat he said, "I've worked on many a flat tire in my day, but I've never seen anything like this one. I'll take you all back home, and see if I can find a mechanic to come out here and fix it."

When he arrived on the scene, a few hours later, the mechanic's language almost turned the air blue when he squatted down and got a look at the tire. He'd informed them he'd have to tow the car back to the garage where he had the tools to "break down the wheel" to get the tire off. "Thank God, they quit making wheels like this after they put out this model," he told them.

Riding beside his dad as they followed the tow truck back into town, Cecil glumly muttered, "I never thought it would ever be this much trouble."

Burrel smiled grimly. "I think you'd better get rid of it, Son. We sure don't want to have this happen again." Watching his car suspended helplessly behind the tow truck, Cecil reluctantly nodded his agreement.

Monday, after the excitement of the weekend, Polly was happy to have Burrel back at work and June and Cecil in school. Savoring the quietness of the empty house, she had barely positioned herself in her favorite chair with a cigarette and her second cup of coffee when the silence was shattered by the sound of loud demanding pounding on the front door.

Startled, she thought, "Now what?" as she reluctantly made her way to the door.

Opening it, she found herself confronted by a small, extremely irate blonde woman. Her first reaction was to close the door on this person's anger. A closer look warned her that this was something she was going to have to deal with.

Mustering as much charm as she could under the circumstances, she faced this woman with a warm smile. "I'm Mrs. Harman. How may I help you?"

"Oh, so you're his mother!" she said in a shrill, strident voice. As she continued to talk, her voice became even louder, sounding as if she were addressing someone on the next block. Polly glanced around to assure herself none of the neighbors were within earshot. To her relief, no one was.

Still trying to maintain a calm demeanor, Polly said, "I think you'd better tell me who you are and what this is all about."

"I'm Jane's mother," the woman announced. "You remember Jane, the girl your son kept out all Saturday night!" she snarled. Her sarcastic manner made her words sound obscene.

Noticing a neighbor across the street stick her head out the door, and forewarned this wasn't going to be a conversation she would want her to overhear, Polly invited her visitor into the house.

Leading her into the living room, she motioned for her to sit on the couch. Offering her a cup of coffee that was rudely declined, Polly said, "I hope you don't mind if I warm mine up." Not waiting for an answer, she went into the kitchen and a few seconds later returned with a steaming mug.

Again settling into her favorite chair, she said, "Alright, now, what were you saying about my son keeping your daughter out all night? Didn't Jane tell you about the flat tire?"

"Flat tire! Flat tire! Now don't tell me you believe that?" she shouted, her voice dripping with venom. "Even if they did have a flat tire, why didn't your son just put on the spare?"

Only the red spot staining each of Polly's cheeks, and the glint in her eyes betrayed her mounting anger as she tried to explain that even the mechanic hadn't been able to change the tire until he'd towed the car into the garage.

As if she hadn't heard a word Polly had said, the woman shrieked, "The fact remains that my daughter and your son spent the night together. Don't tell me a sixteen-year-old boy and sixteen-year-old girl can be together all night without something happening. I'm here to tell you that your son had better marry my daughter, or he's going to be in big trouble!"

"Marry your daughter?" Polly coolly responded. "My son is not going to marry your daughter, or anyone else, until he's good and ready. Even if he wanted to marry your daughter, I'd fight it 'til my dying day. Jane seems nice enough, but Cecil doesn't need a dirty minded mother-in-law."

She hadn't thought it was possible for the woman's anger to increase, but she had reached a point of incoherence, only able to sputter "You... You!"

Continuing relentlessly, Polly demanded to know if Jane had told her something had happened between them. At first, the question only elicited a cold stare, then to Polly's amazement this angry woman burst into tears. As Polly watched, she buried her head in her hands while her small body was racked with sobs.

This turn of events left Polly momentarily speechless. Instead of the combative feelings she'd felt moments before, she was beginning to feel compassion. Giving the woman a moment to compose herself, Polly went into the kitchen, and returned with a cup of coffee. Sitting next to her visitor, she patted her on the shoulder and said, "Here, drink this. Then we can talk."

The woman looked at her through tear-stained eyes, and managed a smile as she took the cup from her outstretched hand. "I'm sorry," she said. "I shouldn't have talked that way. It's just that with Jane's father overseas, it's hard raising her by myself. Jane told me nothing happened, but I was so afraid. What would I tell my husband if something happened to Jane while he was gone?"

"The kids had quite an experience," Polly said. "But it didn't have anything to do with sex. Didn't Jane tell you what happened?"

"Yes, she told me, but I didn't know whether or not to believe her. After all, they were out all night," she said, emphasizing the last four words.

"Have you had problems with Jane lying to you?" Polly asked. This question seemed to surprise Jane's mother.

"No," she responded. "At least, not until now." Then running both hands through her hair, she murmured, "I don't know what to think or believe."

"You can believe Jane," Polly said. "I can assure you, Cecil did have a flat tire. One he couldn't fix. They were miles from town and had to wait until someone came by who could call us. Cecil's father went down to try to change it, but he didn't have any better luck than Cecil had. They ended up getting it towed into the garage. Believe me, I know. They had a flat tire!"

Sighing deeply, Polly's visitor managed a smile when she said, "That's what Jane told me. I guess I should have believed her. It's so hard being a good mother in times like these."

Though she'd only been a mother for a couple years, Polly wholeheartedly agreed. Remembering the fear she'd felt when Cecil hadn't come home, she breathed a prayer of thanksgiving that Burrel had been there with her that night. How must it have been for this woman sitting alone waiting?

After her apologetic visitor departed, Polly thought longingly of her interrupted solitude. She always enjoyed those few moments of Monday morning quiet before beginning her week's work. A few minutes later, balancing the laundry basket on her hip, she headed for the basement, muttering, under her breath, "I'd better get to work if I'm going to get the laundry done before the family gets home."

As she began putting the clothes into the hot soapy water, it occurred to her that no matter how clean and sparkling she got the clothes, what she'd accomplished this morning was far more important in the scheme of things.

By evening, the closets and drawers were full of clean clothes, and Polly had made up her mind, it was time for Cecil to get a different car, and for Burrel to have a little talk with him about girls. She never wanted a repeat of this morning's visit.

~

It was a warm and balmy evening at the end of May nineteen forty-four. June had just settled into her seat to watch a movie at the Grand Theater in downtown Newark when she heard a latecomer walk down the darkened aisle. When the person stopped beside her seat, she was too engrossed in the love scene on the screen to even glance at him as he took the empty seat beside her. All thought of the action on the screen vanished though when a familiar voice whispered her name and she felt a well remembered hand on hers. Several movie goers shushed her as she exclaimed, "Butch, it can't be you! I thought you were still overseas."

Even in the dim light, she could see the laughter in his eyes as he said, "Pinch me if you don't believe I am real." Then as people either smiled at the happy reunion or hissed, "Shhhhh," Butch whispered, "Do you really want to see the rest of the movie or can we go someplace where we can talk? I have to leave in the morning."

She stood up and tugged on his arm as she mouthed. "Let's go." Her hand in his, they walked around the square to their favorite soda fountain where they had banana splits and talked until the lights dimmed to signify that the restaurant was closing. As they walked a few blocks to the house on Lawrence Street, he told her he knew that something big was about to happen. Although he didn't know what it was, he and his shipmates thought it was going to be something really important. "I was given the one night to come home and see my family before we embark, but I didn't want to leave without seeing you," he said.

As they neared the house, June noticed the one light burning in the front window and explained to Butch that her father was working out of state and Polly had gone to visit him. "Since there is only one light on, Cecil isn't home yet, but he will be here any minute." Then for the next hour they sat on the front porch steps and talked about their lives since he had gone to war. When Cecil came home, he plopped down on the lower step and told Butch that he was going to join the navy when he graduated. "What's it like living on a ship?" he asked.

Butch replied. "It's not bad. I'm not on a big battleship. I'm on a Landing Ship Medium or LSM. We've nicknamed it our Landing Ship Men. It's a small flat bottom ship built to land the marines on the beachhead. We head the boat directly into the beach, drop the stern anchor, open the bow doors and lower the ramps so the marines can land."

"Kind of storm the beaches," Cecil quipped.

Butch laughed and replied, "That's not a bad description of it."

Cecil visited for a while until June pointedly glanced toward the door a couple of times. He finally took the hint and sauntered into the house leaving them alone.

With the thought in both their minds that Butch and his shipmates on the LSM ship were heading into danger, they didn't want to say goodnight although Cecil stepped out a few times to ask when she was coming inside. They talked until they were both hoarse and the sun was rising over the rooftops of their neighbors' houses.

Then just as Butch put his arms around her and kissed her goodbye, a neighbor woman stepped onto her front porch and saw them. She loudly cleared her throat to get their attention before she asked, "When is your mother coming home?" When June replied that she would be home in a few hours, the woman firmly stated, "I'll want to see her when she gets here."

June and Butch exchanged glances as they realized the woman had read more into the fact that he had been with her all night than the conversation and harmless kisses that had taken place. Butch put a comforting arm around her before he said, "I won't be here to talk to your mother, but if you think that you are going to be in trouble, I'll be glad to write to her."

June told him that she appreciated the offer, but she wasn't worried about her mother being angry once she knew that they had sat on the porch steps all night. When she got home from school that afternoon, Polly was waiting for her with fire in her eyes, but once she heard June's side of the story, she went so far as to say that not only did she believe her, but that she had always liked Butch and hoped he would come home safely from this terrible war.

Then a couple weeks later, on June 7, the newspapers proclaimed that the allied forces had landed on the beaches of Normandy the day before. On what would always be referred to as D-Day, the navy including LSM crafts like the one Butch was on, was involved in landing thousands of men and tanks as close to shore as possible amidst the gunfire. June knew, as she devoured the news and sat through the newsreel twice that this was the "something big" Butch had anticipated. She was glad she had been able to spend the time with him before he left for battle, though her reputation might have suffered in the eyes of her neighbor because of it.

CHAPTER EIGHTEEN
ROSES ARE RED, JUNE IS BLUE

As days passed and the school year was coming to a close, the family's attention shifted to plans for June's graduation from Junior High School. She would soon officially be a sophomore and Cecil would be a senior in high school. It was hard for Polly to perceive that the children who had come into her life three years before would soon be young adults.

All the girls in June's class were going to wear pastel colored dresses for the graduation ceremony. A powder blue one that June had spent the last few Saturdays admiring in the window of the Betty Gay Dress Shoppe, was now hanging in her closet...ready for the big day.

Priscilla had written to find out what color she would be wearing, so she could send her a corsage. The day before graduation morning, June waited anxiously for the corsage to be delivered. When it still hadn't arrived by the time the florist closed his shop, she couldn't hide her disappointment. It was hard to believe that her mother had broken her promise. "I'll be the only girl there without a corsage," she moaned.

"No, you won't," Polly said. "We'll come up with something. Like June, she could hardly believe Priscilla had let her daughter down. She wasn't sure what she was going to do, but she'd have to think of something.

"You bet we'll think of something," Burrel said that evening as he and Polly discussed it over their after dinner coffee. "I think I saw some roses blooming in Mace's backyard the last time I was over there. I think I'll go and check it out."

Polly watched him amble across the street and return a few minutes later with a bouquet of red roses. She laughed when he asked, "Do you think this will be enough?"

"I'd say that's enough for half a dozen corsages," she replied as she took them from his outstretched hand. This won't look as good as what her mother would have sent, but with this white hair ribbon it should look alright."

"I don't know why they're having the ceremony in the morning. I hate to miss it. I'm sure I'm not the only father who's going to be working," he complained.

June was also disappointed her father wasn't going to be there, but the next morning while standing on the stage, looking out into the audience, she was happy to see Polly sitting in one of the front row seats, smiling and nodding her approval.

As the principal, Miss McDonagh, gave her traditional speech, praising this as the best class to ever graduate from this school, June looked around at her classmates. The girls were pretty in their pastel dresses and white shoes. She was surprised to see that she wasn't the only one wearing a homemade corsage.

She felt a momentary pang at the thought of the one she hadn't received, but reflecting on the love that had gone into this one made her feel proud.

Diploma in hand, she stood smiling while Miss McDonagh called out the names of her classmates. When she heard Albert Hunt's name, she thought about a day a few months before when the two of them had learned a valuable lesson, one she knew she would never forget.

She remembered how she'd felt, that day, in Algebra class when the teacher had written an answer to a problem on the blackboard and asked everyone with that answer to raise their hand.

June could feel her heart sink as every hand except hers and Albert's was raised. While she and Albert exchanged glances, both wondering how they'd gotten it wrong, the teacher erased what she had written and wrote another answer. "Did anyone come up with this answer?" she asked.

Though this was the one she had, June had kept her hands at her side until she saw Albert hesitantly raise his. They both looked embarrassed at the thought of being the only two who had miscalculated it.

June could hardly believe her ears when the teacher said, "This is one time the minority is right." Ignoring moans from the majority, she continued, "Class, I'm glad this happened. It shows that just because the majority holds an opinion, that doesn't necessarily mean it's correct. There will be times in your life when you'll be tempted to go against what you think is right because of what other people think or say. I hope you'll keep this in mind and not be afraid to have your own opinion."

In years to come when June had forgotten the Latin and Algebra she'd learned that year, the one lesson that stayed with her was that even if she were the only one to think a certain way, she could be right.

As she was arriving home after the ceremony, her Aunt Mabel called to her from across the street. "June, come over here. I have something for you."

Curious as to what it could be, June strolled across the street. Handing her a white rectangular box, her aunt said, "This came while you were at the ceremony. Since no one was home at your house, the delivery man left it here."

Opening it, she stared at a corsage of tiny white rosebuds nestled in white tissue paper. Her mother hadn't forgotten! Placed in the folds of the blue bow was a small white card.

June read the neatly printed message. "June, I'll be thinking about you when you graduate tonight." It was signed "Love, Mom." Re-reading the card, the word "tonight" seemed to leap off the page. June was filled with delight, not only because of the beauty of the flowers, but because her mother hadn't forgotten! Somehow there had been a breakdown in communications, with her mother naturally assuming the ceremony would be in the evening.

As she carefully removed the corsage from the box and pinned it next to the one Polly had made, she was momentarily filled with guilt and regret that she'd failed to inform her mother of the time of the ceremony. Though she felt badly about it she wasn't going to allow anything to overshadow her happiness now that she knew her mother hadn't let her down! Even when Rose and Aunt Mabel teased her about looking like a rose garden, she just laughed. She was feeling too good to let anything bother her.

When she got home, Polly was in the kitchen preparing dinner. Proudly displaying her flower-laden dress, June said, "Look what was delivered to Aunt Mabel's this morning."

After properly admiring the new addition to June's apparel, Polly said, "It seems we all jumped to the wrong conclusion. I guess we should have given your mother more credit than we did."

"Yes, I guess so," June replied. "It was all my fault for not telling her it was going to be in the morning. When she said she couldn't come, I didn't give a thought to the time. I guess I didn't think it mattered."

"Don't blame yourself," Polly said. "None of us thought about it. Your mamma will be disappointed when she finds out you didn't get to wear it."

June had been thinking about that too and had already decided what she was going to do. "I'm going to wear it tonight when I go to the graduation party. Then I can honestly write and tell Mom how much I enjoyed wearing it." Sighing deeply, she added, "I don't want her to feel bad about it."

The issue of the late corsage became a case of "What a person doesn't know won't hurt her". Priscilla never asked if it arrived on time, and June never told her.

CHAPTER NINETEEN
TOGETHER AGAIN

After putting the excitement of the graduation behind them, the family turned its attention to Dickie's upcoming visit. Though several times during the school year, June and Cecil had ridden the bus to Mansfield to visit their mother and Dickie, Priscilla had remained adamant that Dickie would have to wait until school was out to come to Newark.

While the house in Newark was filled with anticipation, fifty-five miles away in Mansfield Priscilla didn't share their enthusiasm. As she walked between Dickie's closet and dresser to the open suitcase on his bed where she was carefully packing his clothes, she had to curb her misgivings. Always in the back of her mind was the fear that Burrel would try to keep him.

As she tucked clean socks into the corner of his bag, she thought about the conversation she'd had with Polly last summer. Polly had certainly made it clear she had her hands full with June and Cecil and wasn't planning to take on any more.

A frown creased her forehead when she recalled the panic she'd felt when Polly asked her what Bill would say if she told him she was bringing June and Cecil home to raise. Polly had said she would gladly take Dickie if he didn't already have a mother who wanted him. Priscilla liked to think her husband would feel the same way about her other two children, but that was something they had never discussed.

Burrel and Polly had kept their end of the bargain by letting June and Cecil visit, now despite her misgivings, Priscilla knew she had to keep her end. Putting a smile on her face, she walked downstairs to the living room and called out to Dickie, "It's almost time to leave. If you'll put your bag in the car, I'll see if your dad is ready."

She had felt the need to have her husband with her on this trip. Without the comfort of his presence, she wasn't sure she would be able to drive away leaving her son behind. Bill had talked to her the night before reassuring her that this was going to be alright. She reminded herself, she'd always been a worrier and if she kept it up, she was going to make herself sick.

With Bill driving and Dickie sprawled in the back seat, Priscilla sat comfortably beside her husband. Though she was looking out the window, she wasn't aware of the familiar landscape. Instead pictures flashed through her mind of her three children talking and laughing together when her older children had spent their Christmas and Easter vacations in Mansfield with them.

She thought about how impossible it would have been for a casual observer to tell they had been separated for almost three years. Until she overheard them talking, she hadn't realized how much her children had missed each other. There had been times during those visits when she'd felt a twinge of regret at the thought of the time they'd all lost.

~

Not wanting to dwell on that thought, she leaned back in her seat, closed her eyes and started to reflect on June's friendship with Mrs. Shier, their next-door neighbor. A small, vibrant woman, she drew young people to her like a modern day Pied Piper. This was partly because of the sheer force of her personality, but the rest was due to the dramatic story she had to tell.

Remembering the vivid imagination her daughter had as a child, Priscilla could understand her fascination with this woman. June had first become acquainted with her because of Priscilla's lack of an extra bedroom. Before one of June and Cecil's visits, Priscilla had been bemoaning the fact to her neighbor that June was going to have to sleep on the couch. In response Mrs. Shier had graciously said, "We have a guest room. When she visits why don't you let her stay with us?"

Priscilla had readily agreed, and during future visits, close to bedtime, June would walk the short distance between the two houses and spend the night next door.

While Mr. Shier was working the night shift at one of the local defense plants, June and Mrs. Shier had talked into the small hours of the morning. June had quickly come to admire this courageous woman, as she listened to the dramatic story of her life in Germany and how she'd come to escape from the Nazis. The story of Mrs. Shier and her husband's flight from their homeland rivaled any movie of the war June had ever seen.

A gentile, Mrs. Shier had grown up the pampered daughter of a prosperous family in Berlin. While in college she had met, fallen in love with, and married a young Jewish man. At that time, Adolph Hitler had been a dim figure on the horizon of German politics.

Soon though, they had begun to hear disturbing accounts of his anti-Semitic speeches. The first time they actually heard him, they'd been strolling through the streets close to their home. When they'd seen a crowd gathering, they'd gone over to find out what was going on. They'd soon found themselves in the midst of a mass of people listening to the shouts of a small, inconsequential looking man. With his dark lank hair falling onto his forehead and with his small black mustache, he didn't look like a threat. Instead he looked more like a comic, one she would expect to see in a local cabaret.

Neither she nor her husband had found anything to laugh about when they saw the almost maniacal gleam in his eyes and heard the words of pure unadulterated hatred spewing from his mouth. Mrs. Shier had felt her blood run cold when she'd realized all the hate was addressed against the Jews, her husband's people.

Watching the people surrounding her, she had been even more frightened by their reaction to his frenzied but magnetic oratory. His ranting was constantly being interrupted by their shouts of "Heil Hitler"!

As the months passed, she hadn't been able to erase this picture from her mind. While he'd continued to gain in power, she had found him even more terrifying. Fearful of their future as Jewish people in Germany, Mr. Shier's brother had taken his family and immigrated to New York. Before boarding the ship for New York, he'd tried to convince his brother to come with them.

A stubborn man, he wouldn't even consider it. He felt he had too much tied up in his life in Berlin to just pack up and leave. He owned and operated a shoe factory, and they had just bought a house. He'd told his brother that if things got worse, he'd try to sell everything, and they'd join him in America.

Unfortunately, he'd waited too long. Aware that other Jewish neighbors were being rounded up, herded into boxcars and taken away, Mrs. Shier and her husband had begun to live in fear. One night their deepest fear was realized when they'd been awakened by a knock on their door. They'd crept down the stairs and fearfully opened it. Confronting them on their doorstep was a tall, blonde, blue-eyed man wearing the uniform of the dreaded Gestapo.

All color had drained from Mrs. Shier's face when she saw him standing there. As they'd moved aside, he'd quickly stepped into the entrance hall. Speaking softly, he'd said, "I can only stay a minute." While they stared in open-mouthed wonder, he'd continued, "Now, don't be frightened by my uniform. I am here to help you. You mustn't let anyone know how you found out about it, but you are scheduled to be picked up tomorrow. I've come to warn you. If you want to get away, you need to leave now....Tonight."

As they'd silently stood, their fear still rooting them to the floor, he'd handed Mr. Shier a slip of paper. As they read what was written on it, he continued talking. "Here is the name of someone who can help you get out of the country." As their eyes mirrored their feeling of terror, he'd uttered words of caution, "You mustn't tell anyone about my visit. Until I get caught I'm going to try to save as many people as I can. I can't stand by and see this happen."

Frightened and wary, they'd been unsure whether they should believe him, but one look into his eyes had reassured them. They were full of compassion, something they'd never expected to see in the eyes of a Gestapo officer.

Deciding to trust him, they'd stood in the hallway, listening to him explain how to find the man whose name was on the paper. "He's in the underground. We have a network of people who will help you escape." His use of the word "we" wasn't lost on them. They'd understood. He, too, was a part of the underground movement.

Before slipping out the door, he'd again cautioned them of the dangers to them and their benefactors if they let it slip about his warning or of their impending departure.

Even after their arrival in the United States, they'd remained silent about everything that had happened to them from that night when they'd watched their unlikely rescuer silently disappear into the darkness, until they'd arrived safely in this country.

Though they were now safe in this small Ohio town, they were afraid something they might say could jeopardize the people who had saved their lives. All Mrs. Shier would ever say was that they had escaped with the clothes on their backs and the few personal belongings they could manage to carry with them.

With tears streaming down her cheeks, she had told Priscilla, but not June, one of the most heartrending parts of her story. A few months before their escape, she'd discovered she was going to have a baby. Knowing this child would be born into a hate filled world, she had spent many a soul-searching night before making a very difficult decision. In her mind there was no choice, but to have an abortion. She and her husband had rationalized that when the world was again safe for a child with a Jewish parent, they would have more children.

After arriving in the United States, she discovered this was never to be. As a result of a botched back street abortion, she was barren. Not only was her unborn child a victim of the war, but also any she might have had. Priscilla had often wondered if that explained why she paid so much attention to the neighborhood children.

Bill's comment of, "Don't look so sad. Dickie is going to be fine," brought her back to the present. She had been too engrossed in her thoughts to worry about Dickie's visit.

Her mother had always told her that the best way to forget your troubles was to think about someone else's. This was certainly working for her. Finally becoming aware of her surroundings, she was surprised to see how close they were to Newark.

Her husband and son both wondered what had brought about the change in her attitude when they heard her say, "I'm not worrying anymore. I just want you to have a good time, Son. We'll be back for you in a couple weeks." She refrained from adding, "If you need me, all you have to do is call."

Burrel, still on his overtime schedule, had spent the day of Dickie's arrival bemoaning the fact that he was going to miss the better part of the first day of the visit. These feelings were soon forgotten when he opened the front door that evening and called out his usual greeting, "Hello, everybody. I'm home," and heard the words, "Hi, Dad," coming from his youngest son.

That evening and the next day passed much too quickly, but knowing he'd be working overtime hours during the visit, he managed to cram a world of activities into the weekend. He delighted in showing his younger son around Newark, not even minding using his valuable ration coupons. As he handed the last one to the gas station attendant, he thought, "I'll just have to do a little more car pooling, until the next ration book comes out. I'll make it up to the other drivers next month."

Cecil had a job for the summer, working at the Heisey Glass factory. The hand blown glassware they produced was known world wide for its beauty and fragile appearance. Making it was an art, requiring years of training and practice. His job was as a helper to these artisans. "I'm a flunky!" he laughingly told Dickie. "Whatever they need, I have to get it for them."

In response to Dickie's comment that it must be a fun place to work, Cecil snorted, "Fun? It's hot as Hades! If you've ever stood by an open furnace door, that'll give you an idea of the heat. A lot of my time is spent sweeping up after the men who are blowing the glass. When they shape the piece, they cut off the excess and let it fall to the floor."

"The only good part about it is that I get paid, and they give me seconds to bring home. If they goof up on a piece, it can't be sold. Here's one," he said as he handed Dickie a small crystal horse. Turning it from side to side and examining it Dickie said, "It looks fine to me. What's wrong with it?" Taking it from him, Cecil pointed to an almost indiscernible bubble-like flaw. "I can hardly see it," Dickie said.

"I know," Cecil replied, "but nothing goes out of there with the Heisey trademark on it unless it's perfect." While listening to his brother talk about his working conditions, Dickie wondered aloud why Cecil stayed there.

"It's better than the last place I worked," Cecil exclaimed. He proceeded to tell him about his job with the railroad, and especially the time his dad had made him go to work after he'd been out half the night. "Of all things, that was the time I had a boxcar of frozen coal to dig out and shovel," he moaned.

"After hearing about your jobs, mine selling newspapers doesn't sound too bad," Dickie laughed as he responded. "I'm trying to get a job as a caddie at the golf course. If I don't get hired this summer, I will next."

"If I can tear you guys away from such serious conversation, I thought we'd walk to the grocery store. We can stop at Galleher's drugstore, and I'll buy a coke for each of us," Polly said. "I'll get my purse if one of you will tell June we're ready to go."

She'd barely walked into the bedroom, when she was almost blasted off her feet by their joint bellow, "June, come on we're going downtown."

"I could have done that myself," she said. "I meant for you to go tell her." The words were hardly out of her mouth when June came running down the stairs and into the living room.

The brothers exchanged glances as if to say, "It worked, didn't it?" Not missing the interchange between them, Polly muttered, "You two are as alike as two peas in a pod." To their jaunty expression of thanks, she grinned and retorted, "You're just like your father, and if I hear another of those smart alec thank yous, you can do without your coke." The smile on her face and the twinkle in her eyes took the sting from her words.

Walking along beside her, none of the three took her grumbling seriously. They carried on their lighthearted joshing on their walk downtown, continuing when they'd settled into a booth at the soda fountain.

Although this day was reminiscent of others she'd spent since they'd moved to Newark, having her little brother sitting across from her made it feel special to June. She knew it was impossible, but she couldn't help wishing this visit could last forever.

The waitress came over to their booth and asked what they wanted to order. Without looking at Polly, the three ordered banana splits. "Banana splits?" Polly exclaimed. "I thought we had an understanding you were each going to get a coke."

While the waitress stood, pencil poised, ready to scratch out their order, June explained, "Mom, we worked up an appetite on the walk down here."

The waitress didn't say a word, but her stance and expression clearly showed she was impatient for them to make up their minds. With four sets of eyes upon her, Polly mulled it over before saying, "Why not? After all, this is a special occasion." To everyone's surprise she told the waitress, "Make that four banana splits."

As the waitress moved away, she added, "I was just thinking about the money. This is going to cost me a dollar when I could have gotten the pop for twenty cents, but what the heck? We're celebrating Dickie being here." Turning and addressing him, she added, "These two do this to me all the time. The next time, they're not going to get away with it."

As the waitress sat the gooey looking confections before them, they exchanged glances and grinned. They'd heard that before, but she always relented. Maybe it was because, like a kid herself, she too would rather have a banana split than a coke.

～

The mood was so festive that Polly decided, before they left the drug store, to buy cinnamon balls, June and Cecil's favorite candy. The size and shape of a marble, they were hot and spiced with cinnamon. They all agreed that it was time to introduce Dickie to them.

As they walked down the street to the grocery store, they were each sucking on a piece of the candy. It was so hot that tears sprang to their eyes. "Good, huh?" Cecil laughingly asked. Grinning at Dickie, who was using his hand to fan his burning mouth, Polly told them she figured if anyone saw the three of them, they'd think she'd been beating them. To which Cecil replied, "You'd better look at yourself in one of the store windows, Mom. We're not the only ones who have red faces."

It was a lighthearted group who made their way down the aisles of the grocery store. Armed with her grocery list, a pencil to check off each item, and with ration stamps clutched in her hand, she marched up and down the aisles, picking up some items while discarding others until everything on her list was crossed off. "That's it," she said. "I think we have all we can carry, don't you?"

"Yes, I think we do," June murmured, "But where is Dickie?" To Polly's inquiry as to when she'd last seen him, she replied, "I guess it was when we were looking at the watermelons. I thought he was right behind me, though."

"Go and see if you can find him," Polly instructed. On her way to the back of the store, she spotted him, not two feet from where she'd left him. He was standing beside a large bin piled high with watermelons. Seeing his sister heading toward him, he plaintively asked, "Do you think Polly would get one of these?" Without waiting for an answer, he added, "Don't they look good?"

"Sure they do, but remember, whatever we buy, we have to carry home. Did you forget that Dad has the car?" Polly, who had gotten tired of waiting for them, had left Cecil to stay with the groceries and had come looking for them. Seeing them standing by the watermelons, she had an inkling of what was to come.

"Polly, can we get one?" Dickie pleaded. "These are the first ones I've seen this year." When she didn't immediately respond, he increased his sales pitch to try to convince her of how much everyone in the family would love it. He even reminded her, "I remember how much Dad loved watermelons. Just think how happy he'd be if we had this for him when he got home."

She tried to explain, she would be glad to buy one, but they had a long way to walk, and they would have to carry the watermelon. "I'll carry it," he answered. "I'm strong. I won't have any trouble."

Against her better judgment, she gave in. The dirty looks bestowed on her by people passing by and the words of criticism she overheard when folks saw this small boy lugging such a humongous watermelon, made her wonder if she'd made the right decision. "If looks could kill," she thought, "Burrel would be planning my funeral."

Their steps weren't quite as light on the trip home as they had been on the walk downtown. "We're quite a sight," she mused as they trudged along, arms laden with bags of groceries. Not for the first time, she wished Burrel's job didn't require so many overtime hours. With stores closed on Sunday, his only day off, it certainly made grocery shopping a chore.

Dickie didn't complain, although the strain on his thin arms and back were terrible. He'd made up his mind; he wasn't going to let anyone know how hard it was to carry his heavy load. Every so often, as he put one weary foot in front of the other, the watermelon would begin to slip through his arms, and he'd lift his knee to catch and reposition it. Noticing this and the beads of sweat standing on his forehead, Cecil said, "I'm sure tired of carrying these groceries. How about you toting them for awhile, and let me take the watermelon?"

Although the offer was tempting, Dickie told Polly he could carry it, and barring it slipping from his arms and shattering on the sidewalk, he was going to do it. He managed to put on a brave front, pretending it wasn't even heavy, but when he turned the corner and saw his father's house, he felt like shouting, "Hurray. I made it!"

His earlier prediction proved to be correct. The watermelon was delicious, and they all enjoyed it, especially Burrel. Dickie beamed from ear to ear when he heard his dad say, "Whoever's idea this was, it was a great one! I don't know when I've ever tasted watermelon this good."

He continued to grin in pleasure as he listened to his dad's words and watched the family savoring every bite. "I don't know if I'd ever do it again," he thought. "But seeing Dad enjoy it so much, I'm glad I did manage to get it here...this time."

Later that night after they'd gone to bed, Polly told Burrel about Dickie's determination to carry it himself, and how he wouldn't ask for or accept any help. Her words reminded Burrel of Dickie when he was a little boy, "I can remember," he said. "He was always like that. Once he made up his mind to do something, nothing would stop him." He fell silent and was quiet for so long Polly thought he'd fallen asleep until she heard him murmur, "You know, I'm proud of that boy. He's got gumption."

"I'd say he does!" she replied. "But then, I can't say I've seen a lack of it in any of your kids." She could hear him chuckling softly as she turned over and again tried to go to sleep. Beginning to drift off, somewhere in the state between being awake and falling asleep, she wasn't sure whether she dreamed it or whether she actually heard him softly whisper, "I've missed that boy."

"Yes, Honey. I know you have," was her last thought before she joined him in slumber.

～

The summer seemed to have its fill of hot sultry days, bringing an influx of flies. This seemed to be especially true on the day following their watermelon feast. Watching them buzz around the screen door, Polly had made up her mind she was no longer willing to share her space with them. When Dickie returned to the house after a morning of riding Cecil's bicycle around the neighborhood, she met him on the steps, fly swatter in hand. "How would you like to make a little money?" she asked.

At the sound of the magic word, he said, "Make some money? I'd love to! What do I have to do?" His enthusiasm amused Polly, who went on to explain that she wanted him to get rid of the flies. "I'll pay you one penny for every regular sized one you dispose of and a nickel for the large blow flies."

He attacked the task with fervor, and before the day was over he would earn a pocket full of money. The keenness of his eye and the swiftness of his weapon had earned him a reputation among the flying insects of the neighborhood. The hum that could be heard in the air that afternoon must have been the sound of the word being passed from fly to fly to steer clear of the house at 229 Lawrence Street. That kid, who was visiting there, was too quick for them. Whatever the case, the infestation had been brought to an end.

Polly kept her end of the bargain and handed Dickie a fistful of change. Spreading the nickels and pennies out on the kitchen table, so he could count his earnings, he exclaimed, "Wow! This is great!" Scooping the coins into his pocket, he said, "Everybody's been treating me since I got here. Now it's my turn. Come on, June. Let's go get some ice cream."

The money seemed to be burning a hole in his pocket, so June took pity and walked around the corner with him to Taylor's grocery store. While she chatted with some friends, he took his time pouring over the contents of the shelves of penny candy before returning to his original idea and buying each of them an ice cream cone.

The brother and sister laughed together, on the way home, at the memory of the astonished looks on June's friends' faces when she'd introduced them to her previously unknown "little brother". "I guess they thought they knew all about me," she chuckled. "But I don't let very many people really get to know me. That's a habit I got into when we were moving around so much."

~

To Burrel, this visit had turned out to be everything he'd dreamed it would be. Although he hadn't been able to spend much time with Dickie, the time they'd been together had taken on an extraordinary importance. Even the most mundane activity had been special to him, simply because his youngest son was with them.

The day arrived much too soon when Priscilla was to come and take Dickie home. Burrel found himself dreading the thought that when he got home from work that day, Dickie's familiar greeting of "Hello, Dad" would be missing.

Early that morning, while he was lamenting this fact to Polly, over his breakfast coffee, he heard footsteps on the stairs and a sleepy voice from the doorway say, "Dad."

He turned his head and saw Dickie, tousle haired, rubbing the sleep from his eyes. "I didn't expect to see you this morning, Son. I figured you'd want to sleep in."

"That bed felt pretty good," Dickie said. "But I'll be gone when you get home. I just wanted to say goodbye, before you had to go to work."

A soft gentle smile played across Burrel's face as he stood up and put his hands on his son's thin shoulders and said, "It's been great having you here, Son. I'll miss you."

"I'll miss you, too, Dad," Dickie said. "But I'll be back." Then with a mischievous look in Polly's direction, he added, "Polly might need my services...if the flies come back."

This brought a laugh from the three of them, and Burrel carried its echo with him as he left the house and drove to work. His smile was tinged with sadness though when he caught a glimpse, in the rear view mirror, of his son and wife waving from their spot on the front porch. That night, after Priscilla had taken Dickie home, when June went to her room, she sat on the bed, looking at the picture her mother had given her. Her own reflection was imposed upon the framed, glass-covered portrait of herself, her mother and brothers. She smiled at the faces smiling back at her, as she remembered the difficulty the photographer had trying to get all of them to smile at once. "Hold that smile," he'd commanded. "Now don't close your eyes!" he'd groaned.

Her smile broadened when she remembered how their relief had mingled with laughter when he'd tripped out of the room muttering, "That's it! I got it! Finally!" He had been mistaken as they were to find out when they saw the proofs. While Priscilla, Cecil, and Dickie were smiling, June's expression had been pensive. The photographer had unknowingly caught her innermost feeling of wonder that the four of them were again together.

Placing the picture on her bedside table where it would be the last thing she saw before she went to bed and the first thing she'd see in the morning, she turned off the light and slipped under the sheet.

Looking out the window at the star filled sky, her thoughts turned from the day they'd had that picture taken to the visit with Dickie that had just ended. She reflected on how long they had all waited for his visit and how quickly the time had gone by. Though her mind told her they would see each other when she and Cecil visited in Mansfield, in her heart she knew it wouldn't be the same. During the time he'd been here she'd almost been able to convince herself things were the way they'd been when they'd lived together as a family in Petersburg.

Her thoughts were in turmoil, wandering first to the time when they had been a different family and then to the years in between. She remembered when she'd been younger, she'd thought she had a perfect family, and that this was a perfect world. Now she knew neither of these beliefs had been true, and she knew she had to come to terms with the changes the years had brought.

While she recalled the family they'd been, she decided it was time to concentrate on the one they'd become. No longer the unblemished family circle, they were none-the-less a family. Now the circle was battered, stretched, pulled out of shape, with a dent here and a bump there. While the circle was no longer shiny, it had expanded to let the new family members in. As a cloud obscured the moon, throwing June's room into total darkness, she was too deep in her thoughts to notice.

"We are a family!" she thought. "We'll never be what we were, but what we are is fine. Cecil and I will get to see Mom and Dickie at their house, and Dad will get to have Dickie spend time with us." The last thought to flicker across her mind before she fell asleep was, "Maybe things aren't perfect, but everything is better now then it was a few months ago."

CHAPTER TWENTY

THE SURPRISE PACKAGE

Downstairs in their bedroom Polly and Burrel were sitting propped up in bed. Burrel was talking about his younger son's visit. "Having Dickie here made me feel like I did when I was a kid and found what I'd been asking for under the Christmas tree," he said.

They talked about the success of the visit, until Burrel began to feel drowsy and relaxed. Positioning his pillow just the way he liked it, he had just gotten himself comfortably settled and ready to drift off to sleep when he heard Polly say, "You know how everything I've been eating lately has been making me sick?"

His voice sounded sleepy but was full of concern as he replied. "Yes, I remember. You said you thought it was from that lunchmeat you'd eaten. Cecil said, the other morning after I went to work, you were throwing up. You're not still doing that, are you?"

"I sure am!" she declared. "And I knew he heard me, because afterwards he was teasing me about hugging the toilet. I felt too miserable to be amused. Then June saw me and said, "Mom, I bet you're pregnant." I was so mad at her, that I threw a wet washcloth at her! I hit her, too," she proudly exclaimed.

Any feeling of drowsiness had left Burrel when he heard the word "Pregnant." "Pregnant, you're not pregnant?" he cried. "You told me the doctor said you couldn't have any children. How could you be pregnant?"

"I'd say it happened in the usual way. You're a big boy now. You figure it out!" she snapped. Then in a softer tone she continued, "I went to the doctor today, and he said I definitely am going to have a baby, and it will be here in late January or early February. I'm as surprised as you are. You know as well as I do, I've been told by several doctors that because of the way my uterus is tilted, I'd never be able to conceive. Obviously, they were wrong." Then near tears, she added, "Aren't you the least bit happy about my news?"

"Of course, I'm happy. It's just that it's such a surprise," he replied. Even to his own ears his response hadn't sounded sincere.

Deep furrows had formed in his brow when he again spoke, "In August, I'll be forty one years old. Maybe I'm getting too old to start all over again," he said. "Cecil will be graduating in a year and June a couple years after that. I guess, I was thinking about the two of us having some time together when they were grown. I wasn't thinking about raising another family."

Turning off the light and moving closer to him, she murmured, "From the way I've been feeling, I'd say you're not the least bit too old to be a daddy." Then sighing softly, she added, "I understand how you feel, though. It was a shock to me too, but now that I've had a chance to think about it, I like the idea of us having a little one of our own."

She was quiet for such a long time, he thought she'd fallen asleep until he heard her quietly murmur, "I think I would like a little blonde, blue-eyed girl, one who'll look like you."

"Wait a minute," he said. "We already have a blue-eyed, blonde girl. I think I'd like a little redhead, like you." She liked hearing that. It was beginning to sound as if he were getting used to the idea. Lying quietly beside her as she slept, he listened to her soft breathing and thought of how vulnerable she seemed. As he propped himself up on his elbow and looked down at her sleeping face, he was overcome with pangs of remorse for the way he'd responded to her news. He reasoned that since she had so completely taken over as June and Cecil's mother, it hadn't occurred to him she'd want a baby. "She had never even hinted that she wanted children," he mused. Now that he thought about it, though, he could understand how, as young as she was, she would want a child of her own. He amended that thought to "child of our own".

He slept fitfully that night, and woke as the early morning light was coming through the bedroom windows. Not wanting to wake her, he crept out of bed and into the kitchen where he put the coffee pot on the back burner. When he saw steam pouring from its spout, he filled his mug and carried it to the front porch. Sitting, sipping his coffee and listening to the birds burst forth in their early morning song, he thought about the events of the last couple weeks.

First, his most fervent wish had been granted, Priscilla had let his youngest son come to visit. For the first time since the divorce, she didn't seem to be afraid he'd try to keep Dickie. From now on, he felt certain she would be letting him visit often. It had made him happy seeing his three children together. At times during these last two weeks, he'd almost felt as if they'd never been apart.

Now he had this latest news from Polly about her pregnancy. He was aware this wouldn't make much difference in June and Cecil's lives. They'd be grown in a few years, but it certainly would be a change in his and Polly's. "When I was in my twenties it was easy being a father of a little one, but how will I do now that I'm in my forties?" he wondered.

As he continued to sip his coffee, he realized he and the birds seemed to have the neighborhood to themselves. If people were stirring, it must be inside their houses. He hadn't seen another soul since he stepped out onto the porch. Occasionally, he'd hear a dog barking in the distance, and the birds continuing with their merry songs. This solitude was a perfect background for his meandering thoughts.

Peering across the street, he couldn't quite see the small white cottage nestled in the trees at the rear of his brother's house. It was clearly visible, though, in his mind's eye, not as it was now, but as it had been when he and Priscilla had first set up housekeeping within its four walls. They had been so young, so confident that life was always going to be as good to them as it had been then. Echoing in his mind were other pictures. He could recall the fear and excitement he'd felt when Pricilla's mother Rhoda placed his first born in his reluctant arms. Vividly, he remembered a very young, very angry Priscilla meeting him at the door of his father's house demanding that he take her, little Cecil, and newborn baby "Mildred" away from there…that very minute!

Closing his eyes and letting his thoughts continue to wander, June and Cecil's excitement when the merry-go-round seemed to spring up overnight in their front yard at the cavern was as real to him as it had been that day so long ago. He could feel himself protectively standing on the carousel beside two-year-old June. He remembered smiling at Priscilla, who was riding beside four-year-old Cecil who was pretending to be a cowboy astride a fierce looking wooden carnival horse. His feelings that day of how lucky he was to have this wonderful family and a job he loved, flashed into his mind, as real as they had felt then.

Mixed in with his happy memories were the unhappy ones: his illness, the death of his mother and both of Priscilla's parents, the searing pain when he was shot, and the different kind of pain he'd felt when he had to leave the job at the cavern. Through these difficult times, he and Priscilla had seemed to draw strength from each other. No matter what had happened, he'd felt that together they could handle it.

He was overwhelmed with a sense of sadness when he remembered the dark time when Priscilla left and his life had fallen apart. He had felt as insecure during those months as he had been confident during the earlier times in his life. As he sat pondering the past, he knew deep within his being that there were things he should have done differently. He had been lifted from the depth of that despair, though, when he had found a new love and made a new life with Polly and the children. "Life is full of surprises," he reflected.

His reverie was interrupted by the sound of the milkman's truck stopping in front of the house and the milkman calling out, "You're up pretty early aren't you, Mr. Harman? I'm not used to seeing anyone out when I make my rounds."

Replying that it was a little early, even for him, Burrel took the milk bottles from his hands and after discussing the weather for a few minutes went inside and put them into the refrigerator. Peeking into their bedroom, and seeing that Polly was still asleep, he helped himself to another cup of coffee and returned to his solitary spot on the porch.

Now his thoughts turned to Polly's news. He could imagine the reaction of the guys he worked with when they heard that he was going to be a daddy again. Some of those young whippersnappers treated anyone over thirty like an old man. A slow grin spread across his face when he thought, "This will show them what an 'old man' can do."

His thoughts turned serious and he felt a sense of guilt as he remembered how unenthusiastically he'd responded to Polly's announcement. "I don't want to let her down," he thought. "She's always been there for me and the kids when we've needed her." He had a feeling that the reason he'd reacted the way he had was because he'd always been afraid this marriage, too, might fail. The thought of ever losing another child, as he had Dickie, was unbearable.

He knew he was going to have to make it up to Polly for his half-hearted response to her news. The time he'd spent this morning reflecting on his life with Priscilla and the mistake he'd made in not being responsive to her needs, had made him realize he didn't want to make the same mistake again. He knew he needed to be sensitive with Polly at such an important time in her life. "In both our lives," he thought.

"Maybe this little person wasn't planned, but I'm going to see that it receives a big welcome, as big as the other three had," he murmured. As he sat contemplating the future, a feeling of excitement began to course through him. He was reminded of his days of exploring caverns in West Virginia when every twist and turn brought something new and exciting.

The prospect of discovering new places and meeting strangers had always appealed to him. What could be more exciting than this new person coming into their lives? He chuckled quietly when he thought about the prospect of a fiery redhead, like its mother. Smiling ruefully he silently wondered, "Will I be able to keep up with two Polly Wally Wampus Cats?"

～

Engrossed in his thoughts, he hadn't heard the door open and June silently step onto the porch, until she asked, "What are you doing out here at this time of morning?"

"I couldn't sleep, so I just came out to listen to the birds and to think," he responded. "Come over here and sit with me for a spell." Accustomed to hearing her mother coax her every morning to get out of bed, he was surprised to see her. "I didn't wake you, did I?" he asked.

"No," she replied. "I just didn't sleep very well. I've been thinking about Dickie being here, and how much I hated to see him go home. These last two weeks went by so fast, I can't believe they're over."

"It's hard for all of us, but you know we need to enjoy what time we can be together. I hated not being able to see him all those years, and I know how bad it was for you kids to be separated. We can't dwell on that part of our lives." His voice was soft and reassuring when he added, "What we have to do is appreciate what we have now."

Sitting beside her father and listening to him speak was making her feel better. Treasuring any time she spent with him, she reflected upon how much she appreciated knowing he was always there when she needed him. Even when he couldn't be physically present, she knew she could count on him.

"Are you upset because Dickie went home?" June asked. "Is that why you couldn't sleep?" Looking into her somber blue eyes, he wondered how much he should tell her about Polly's news. Sensitive to his apparent apprehension, June searched his face. Unable to understand his enigmatic expression, she hesitantly asked, "What is it, Dad? What's going on?"

His smile moved slowly across his face causing his eyes to sparkle and dance as he replied, "Yes, I have been thinking about that, but I've been thinking about something else, too." His smile seemed to expand as he asked, "Do you remember when your mom got mad and hit you with a wet wash cloth? Do you remember what you said that made her throw it at you?"

"She's going to have a baby?" June cried. "I was right. Oh, wow! She is going to have a baby!" Excited, she was laughing in pure happiness. "I knew she had morning sickness!" she exclaimed. "That's just wonderful!" she added.

In a serious sounding voice, he quipped, "I don't know how pleased she'll be to hear that you think it's wonderful she has morning sickness." June started to explain what she'd meant, but was interrupted by his chuckle, making her realize he'd been teasing her.

"What's going on out here?" Polly called from the doorway. "I know you're an early bird," she said to Burrel, "But what's this sleepyhead doing up?" she asked. Surprised by the flash of June's radiant smile and Burrel's mischievous grin, she added, "You two look like the cat that swallowed the canary. What have you been talking about?"

"Not much," June innocently replied. "We were just talking about wet wash cloths and stuff like that." Polly's glance shifted from one to the other before settling on her husband's face. Her lips silently formed the words, "She knows?"

To his affirmative nod, she looked inquiringly at June before saying, "Well, what do you think? Are you ready for a little brother or sister?"

June laughed as she pretended to check Polly's hands for the presence of any wet washcloths, before replying, "I think it's wonderful." All the questions, she hadn't yet had a chance to ask, began pouring from her mouth. "When is it due? How are you feeling? What are we going to call her?"

"Her?" Burrel asked. "What makes you think it will be a girl? You know, you could have another brother." June and Polly both exchanged glances that said, "A lot you know!" They had made up their minds; it was going to be a girl. Polly was sure it would be a blue-eyed blonde. June, like her father, was looking forward to a little redhead.

No sooner had Burrel said, "In another seven months, we'll know," then a sleepy voice from inside the house asked, "Know what?" The owner of the voice ambled onto the porch, running his hands through his tousled hair. "Why is everyone up so early? I could hear you talking and June laughing all the way upstairs in my room."

Polly looked at her oldest son and replied, "I guess I might as well put an ad in the paper! I hadn't planned to tell everyone yet, but there's no keeping anything secret around here." Her smile and light tone belied the curtness of her words. "If you must know," she announced, "I'm going to have a baby."

"Oh, that. With all that throwing up you were doing, I figured that out a long time ago," Cecil replied. While they all stared at him, he turned and sauntered toward the front door. Before disappearing from their view, he turned and asked, "What's for breakfast?"

To their explosive response, he grinned wickedly and said, "Only kidding! It's great news, Mom. When's he due?" After Polly had filled them in on all the details, Cecil added his prophesy to the rest of the family's, "It'll probably be another girl, but I hope it's a boy."

Some good-natured bickering followed with all except Cecil wanting a girl. Before the morning was over, they'd settled on a name. "I've always wanted to name my daughter after Mamma," Polly said. "Marguerite Louise."

"Marguerite Louise?" Burrel echoed. "That's nice, just so she's not called Maggie, like your mom." Polly assured him that would never happen.

June agreed with her dad. This baby was going to be special and needed a name of its own. "I like the nickname Margi for Marguerite," she said. Polly liked it too, and Burrel would have agreed to anything to keep his daughter from being called Maggie. Watching his son help himself to another stack of pancakes, Burrel marveled at the amount of food a teenaged boy could put away. "It'd better be a girl," he jokingly declared. "I don't know whether I would be able to feed another growing boy."

Cecil, used to being kidded about his appetite, ignored the comment and concentrated on consuming every morsel on his plate before replying, "I think we'd better think of a boy's name, just in case."

During the next few months, many friends and family members repeated the statement, but Polly turned a deaf ear. This baby she was carrying was Marguerite Louise, and no one was going to make her think otherwise.

As determined as she was to have her own way, fate was even more determined, and little Margi was never to make her debut into their lives.

Polly's morning sickness proved to be a forerunner of the difficulties she was to encounter during this pregnancy. Before it was over she had developed a condition called placenta previa, causing her to spend months in bed. On one of her visits to the doctor, he had informed her that she would have to be very careful if she wanted to bring this baby to full term. His warning had frightened her into following his directions explicitly.

Polly's mother responded to a plea for help by traveling from Mississippi to spend the last few months of the pregnancy caring for her. This pampered southern woman, used to having domestic help, valiantly tried, but it was no easy task for her. Dealing with Polly's new family, the snow, and the large house that never seemed to be warm enough for her made Nanny feel like a stranger in a strange country.

Having a grandmother in the house was a new experience for June and Cecil, especially when Nanny began taking her grandmotherly duties seriously. The first time this happened, June was sitting at her dressing table daydreaming over the two photographs she had tucked into her mirror. The first picture was of her blond boyfriend, Butch, and the second was a publicity shot of Tyrone Power, a dark-haired young movie actor, whom she considered very handsome.

She hadn't heard Nanny pad into the room until she heard her say, "That blond young man looks like a nice boy, but I don't like the looks of the dark-haired one. I'd say he's up to no good. In my day, we called eyes like that young man has bedroom eyes."

June smothered a giggle when Nanny added, "Besides, he's much too old for you. Unless you promise me that you won't go out with him, I think I'd better talk to your father about that young man."

With a perfectly straight face, June replied, "You won't have to say anything. I promise never to go out with Tyrone Power."

Satisfied with her response, Nanny left the room. Later when June shared this experience with her brother, he quipped, "I bet if she saw my pin-up picture of Betty Grable in her bathing suit, she wouldn't want me to date her because of her sexy legs." He went on to tell her that Nanny had scolded him about his taste in reading when actually he'd been reading a required book for a book report.

June said, "She caught me with one that I'd checked out of the library the other day, but unlike yours, it wasn't on any required list. When I came home from school last Tuesday, I came in and plopped my books on the table in the hall like I always do, and headed for the kitchen for a snack. When she joined me a few minutes later, she was holding the book. The tight lipped expression on her face made it clear what she thought of my taste in reading. She let me know that in her day girls only read books that would improve their minds. Then she asked if I thought this book would do that for me."

"I was tempted to flippantly reply that I was sure it wouldn't, but it would be a fun read. Mom shook her head for me to drop it, and I did."

"What was the book?" Cecil asked.

"Mildred Pierce," June replied.

Her brother whistled, "In that case, Nanny is probably right. That book is too old for you."

"Et tu," June scoffed. "I picked it up because the main character's name is Mildred like my first name."

"Sure," Cecil grinned teasingly, "Nanny might buy that, but I wouldn't try to get that one by Mom."

June never admitted to her brother or Nanny, but when she read the book she realized that they had been right.

A few days later, June told Cecil, "I really like Nanny. I love to listen to her talk about the social life in Jackson when she was a little older than I am now and was best friends with the governor's daughters. I can only imagine what it would be like to go to parties and dances in the governor's mansion. The way she tells it reminds me of what I expected the South to be like when we moved there. Sort of like Gone With The Wind."

"That was when she was a girl. Things have changed since then," Cecil said. "I know that it has been hard for her coming up here, especially in the winter, but she's been a good sport about it."

June responded "It's been good for Mom having her here. Good for me too. I finally get to know what it's like to have a grandmother, even if she isn't the cookie baking kind. I think that after being here she has a little more respect for Damn Yankees, even if she still thinks we talk funny." June sighed before she added, "Sometimes I feel that we are taking care of two helpless women, she and Mom." Despite some frustrating moments, though, they somehow managed to muddle through.

~

The night Burrel took Polly to the hospital, Polly's mother and June sat up together waiting for news. When midnight came and went without them hearing anything, Polly's mother could no longer stay awake. "You'd better turn in, too," she'd told June as she headed up the stairs to the guest room. June followed her upstairs and tried to sleep, but found that no matter how hard she tried, her vivid imagination would not let her.

The fact that she'd heard nothing, in her mind, meant bad news. If she had been a cursing person, she would have had some choice words for the hospital's rule that no one under sixteen was allowed to visit. While she was mentally composing a searing epitaph, her door opened so quietly, that if her senses had not been so alert she might not have heard it.

Seeing her raise her head and look toward the door, her father whispered, "I didn't want to wake you. I just wanted you to know she's alright. The doctor said it would be a little while yet. I'm going to have some coffee. Then I'm going back to the hospital."

Though their house on Lawrence Street was less than two blocks from the hospital, and he knew he could be there in a matter of minutes, he stayed only long enough to gulp down a cup of coffee before rushing back. Worried as she was, June had to smile at the sight of her usually smoothly shaven dad in the role of a stubble faced expectant father.

He had no sooner rejoined the other nervous men in the waiting room when a nurse stepped through the door and told him that Polly had been "put to sleep", and it would only be a matter of minutes before he'd be a new father. The minutes seemed more like hours before she returned and said, "The baby is here, and your wife is going to be fine."

"What did she have?" he asked. When she told him, he smiled before inquiring, "When can I see her?" Since none of his other children had been born in a hospital, he was surprised and dismayed to hear the nurse recite the long list of the hospital's rules. One that immediately caught his attention was that the new mother would not be allowed visitors for twelve hours after the delivery.

"That doesn't apply to the father, does it?" he anxiously inquired.

The nurse gave him a sympathetic smile before replying, "I'm sorry, Mr. Harman, but it applies to everyone. Your wife needs some time to rest. You've been up all night, too. Why don't you go home and get some sleep yourself." She didn't add, "You look like you could use it," but the glance he caught of his reflection in a mirror on the way through the lobby clearly demonstrated that if she had said it, she would have been right.

Although his opinion of these regulations closely matched what his daughter had been thinking earlier, he knew trying to fight them would have been like beating his head against a wall. With these thoughts in his mind he hurried home and told his anxiously waiting son, daughter, and mother-in-law about the newest addition to the Harman family.

Back in the maternity ward Polly awakened from the cloud of anesthesia she'd been under to a room filled with sunshine. It took a few seconds for her to realize she was no longer in the delivery room. Lifting the sheet, she looked at her belly and gently ran her hands across it to see if it were flat.

She hadn't realized she was not alone until she heard a chuckle from the woman in the next bed. "Yes, you've had your baby. They brought you back hours ago. You've been sleeping like a baby yourself."

Trying to focus her sleepy eyes on the speaker, Polly asked, "Do you know what I had?" Not giving her a chance to respond, she plaintively inquired, "Do you know when I'll get to see her?" The woman smiled sympathetically before explaining that she didn't know anything other than that no one got to see her baby for twelve hours. Then Polly said, "After waiting nine months, I don't know if I can wait any longer. Why do they do that?"

In response, her roommate sighed before uttering the words Polly soon came to hate, "Hospital regulations."

Still groggy from the ether, Polly tried to fight its effects, but she kept drifting in and out of sleep. One advantage to this was that it did help the time appear to go faster.

The words, "Mrs. Harman, there's someone here you'll want to see," intruded into her dream of holding her blonde, blue-eyed Marguerite Louise. She had been enjoying this dream so much; she resented being interrupted by a visitor. This feeling quickly changed when she looked up and saw a white clad figure standing beside her bed holding a small bundle. Her resentment quickly changed to joy.

"Give her to me," she commanded. Accustomed to the impatience of new mothers after the enforced twelve-hour waiting period, the nurse smiled patiently as she moved to the side of the bed and gently placed the bundle in Polly's outstretched arms. As the new mother gently unwrapped the blanket that had been partly obscuring the baby's head, the first thing she saw was the red hair. Below that was a face of almost the same hue. "Well, Marguerite Louise, your daddy got his wish, his little redhead," she murmured.

Raising her eyes to the nurse's face, she thought she saw a look of pity. Fighting to overcome the sudden surge of fear the look had brought, she anxiously asked, "There's nothing wrong, is there? She's okay, isn't she?"

The nurse smiled reassuringly before responding, "Your baby is fine. I can attest to a strong set of lungs, but it's a he, not a she."

Polly was surprised to realize how happy those words made her feel. "A boy," she murmured. "I really wanted a girl, but you'd be surprised how unimportant that all seemed when I thought there might be something wrong with the baby."

As she looked down at his tiny features, a gentle smile played across her face. Except for the red hair, she was looking at a miniature of her husband. "Well, Little Fellow, your daddy wanted a redhead, and I wanted one who looked like him. Aside from your water works, we both got what we wanted," she said.

∼

After the new father was permitted to view his son through the nursery glass, he was finally allowed to see his wife. Knowing how much she'd had her heart set on a girl, he approached her room with much trepidation. She appeared to be sleeping when he walked into the room, but when he neared the bed she opened her eyes and smiled at him. Leaning over he gently kissed her before asking, "How are you feeling, Honey?"

"I'm just great!" she said. Her words and her radiant smile reassured him. She appeared as happy with the new arrival as he was.

By the time visiting hours were over, and he and Polly's roommate's husband were unceremoniously ushered out, the baby had a name, James Fred.

When the new father got home he was greeted by a profusion of questions. "Wait a minute," he said. "Let me answer one at a time." Then, he answered them, one by one. "Polly is doing fine. She doesn't seem to be disappointed that we had a boy. She misses everyone. I saw the baby through the glass. His hair is red. So is his face." With a mischievous glance at his attentive audience, he asked, "Did I answer all your questions?"

"The name! What did you name him?" June cried, in exasperation. Polly's mother and Cecil quickly echoed her question.

Burrel chuckled before replying, "Oh! Did I forget to tell you the name?" Seeing that he was teasing them and enjoying keeping them in suspense, June and Cecil sat grinning at him, but Polly's mother was beginning to show her impatience.

He looked into his mother-in-law's glistening eyes, and in a proud voice announced, "We named him James Fred, after Polly's brother. That was the only name she would even consider."

They all agreed that it was a fine name. Especially elated with their choice, was the new grandmother. "That's wonderful! I didn't know she was going to name it after her brother Fred!"

She was taken aback by the peels of laughter her comment brought, until Burrel reminded her that her daughter hadn't allowed anyone to even mention the possibility that this baby might be a boy.

"How does she feel about it now?" she asked.

"She seems to be really happy," he replied.

"One thing I learned a long time ago was that the good Lord knows better than we do what's good for us. We just have to learn to accept His will," she stated.

"From the expression on her face, when the nurse said she was bringing him in to her, I think she is happily accepting His will," Burrel responded. From the proud look on her father's face, June could tell he wholeheartedly agreed.

CHAPTER TWENTY-ONE
WORDS TO REMEMBER

Later, after Polly's mother had retired for the night and Cecil had gone out with his friends, June and her father remained in the living room, sitting side by side in companionable silence. They both seemed to be absorbed in their own reflections until Burrel said, "A penny for your thoughts."

"I was just thinking about Mom and the baby," she replied. "I was so scared last night that something might go wrong." When he acknowledged that he'd felt the same, she timidly asked, "Dad, were you disappointed that you didn't get a daughter?"

His quiet smile lingered as he softly said, "I have my daughter. I have you. From the first time I saw you, I've been proud to say you're my daughter. I'm perfectly satisfied."

June couldn't think of any present her father could have given her that would have made her as happy as the words she'd just heard. They sat talking for hours, about what their life had been, was now, and would be in the future.

"It's been an interesting journey," her dad said, "And I'm sure the rest of it will be even more so." If he'd had a crystal ball, he would know that before baby Freddy began to crawl, Polly would announce another baby on the way. They would be so close in age, that it would sometimes seem like raising twins. Little red-haired Freddy and black-haired Billy would be ornery little boys who would bring much commotion and love into his life. Yes, life certainly did hold surprises around each corner.

Oblivious of what the future would bring, Burrel's mind was on the past when he said, "During my exploring days I found some mighty interesting things around the next bend in the road. The things I discovered certainly weren't always what I thought they'd be." Then with a rueful grin, he added, "Some I'd just as soon have done without."

He sat quietly, reflecting upon the past, before continuing, "I'm not worried about you or your brothers. You're all good kids. You've come through some rough times, but given the pioneer stock you come from, that's to be expected."

For the briefest of seconds, a distant look crept across his face as if he were looking into the future. "You're fifteen years old now. Before long, you're going to be grown up and leading a life of your own. I feel confident that when you do leave home, you'll do fine. I'm sure, whatever's waiting around that next bend for you, you will be a match for it."

Looking into her somber blue eyes, his voice sounded pensive as he reached over and patted her hand. "Just remember," he said, "Some good can always come out of the bad times. If your mother hadn't left us, Polly and the little fellow would never have come into our lives." Even though his last statement startled her, it didn't take much thought for her to realize it was true. Though she knew she would always be sorry for the years she'd missed with her mother and Dickie, she couldn't imagine her life without this sometimes tempestuous, but more often, compassionate woman.

Before saying goodnight, she hugged him and said, "I'm glad we have them, and also happy Mom and Dickie are back in my life. I wouldn't want to do without any of them."

Later that night, sitting before her dressing table slowly running the brush through her hair, she allowed his words to run through her mind. Although she didn't know it then, those words were to remain with her for years to come.

Many times in the future, both during the good times and the bad, what he'd said that night and the feelings his words had evoked, would unrepentantly return, and she would again feel herself as she was then, three days past her fifteenth birthday, talking to her father in the house on Lawrence Street.

When this happened, she would only have to close her eyes to feel his presence and find comfort, no matter how far apart they might be... as the memories floated, softly and gently, as echoes in her mind.

EPILOGUE

Many momentous events took place in their personal lives and the world around them before they moved from the house on Lawrence Street.

Dickie made them all proud when he became a valuable player on his school's football, baseball and basketball teams. Burrel and Polly's second child, William Cecil, was conceived. Cecil graduated from high school and joined the navy where he remained for twenty-two years. June met the man who was to become her husband.

The nation was saddened when Franklin Delano Roosevelt, who had been elected for an unprecedented fourth term as president, died three months after his inauguration. His feisty vice president, Harry S. Truman, assumed office.

The war in Europe ended following Germany's surrender and the suicide of Adolph Hitler. People were happy and relieved, but celebrations were restrained since the country was still at war with Japan.

Three months later Newark erupted into the biggest celebration its residents had ever seen when the end of the war with Japan was announced. The carnage June had worried about as a child and teenager was finally over. The world was at peace for the first time in nearly a decade.

The men who had so valiantly fought these wars began returning home to resume their lives as civilians. Little did June know one of those men held the key to her future.

PREVIEW OF

Along Came A Soldier

The Third Book in the Echoes In My Mind Series

Along Came A Soldier takes the Harman family from the Post World War II years into the Space Age.

CHAPTER ONE

June noticed the young soldier as he walked toward her. A curvaceous blond clung to his arm while an older dark-haired woman walked sedately beside them. "Isn't that sweet? He's brought his girlfriend and his mother to the movie," she thought. When they stopped at her concession stand, she found his friendly somewhat flirtatious manner puzzling, though. "Hmm," she murmured under her breath as she watched the trio disappear from her sight. For a brief moment, she looked into the darkness and wondered about them. Then she busied herself with other customers and didn't give them another thought.

~

For the last few months, June had been working at the Midland and Auditorium Theaters in downtown Newark, Ohio. She had started at The Midland as an usherette. After a short time, she was given the job to work the concession stand at the Auditorium, The Midland's sister theater. While the new job hadn't offered an increase in her twenty-five cents an hour salary, it had included a whopping commission of ten percent. This had amounted to a penny for each box of popcorn she popped, boxed and sold. When movies starring cowboy star Roy Rogers and his love interest, Dale Evans, were shown, June could actually sell one thousand boxes for the grand sum of ten dollars in commission.

The job offered two perks that she considered as valuable as the money she made. She could attend any movie at either theater free of charge. Most importantly, though, her position in the lobby afforded her a front row seat to the comings and goings in her small part of the world.

Four months earlier, Newark had joined the rest of the country in a massive celebration of the end of World War II, the war that for so long had engulfed the major part of the world. Now the men who had fought so bravely were returning home to get on with their lives. For many of them, this meant getting reacquainted with the women they had left behind.

Always a romantic, June would often stand behind the counter and watch the happy young couples surge through the lobby and imagine romantic scenarios about each one. In her mind's eye, every young couple who passed by was part of a bittersweet story of young lovers who had been separated by this long agonizing war. As she had done many times, she sighed at the thought of the soldier and his girl finally being reunited.

She was so deep in her daydream that she was startled when she heard a male voice say, "Hi there! How about some more popcorn?"

Turning toward her customer, she was surprised to see the dark haired soldier. "Back so soon?" she said. "You certainly haven't eaten three boxes of popcorn already, have you?"

He grinned mischievously at this statement and the tone of her voice before he teased, "You'd better not let your boss hear you say that. He might think you are trying to cut back on sales."

She quickly glanced around to be sure Mr. Tysinger, the theater manager, hadn't heard her comment. Assured he was nowhere in sight, she returned the young man's gaze and in her most dignified manner asked, "How may I help you?"

His grin had widened and there was a sparkle in his brown eyes when he replied, "I'll have three more boxes of popcorn and a date with you." Astonished by his last four words, June was momentarily speechless. Only a few minutes ago he had walked in with two girls, and now he was asking her for a date!

While he stood waiting for an answer, she boxed the popcorn and handed it to him. "That will be thirty-one cents," she said.

He placed three dimes and a penny in her outstretched hand and said, "I also asked for a date. How about it?"

Her smile matched his as she quipped, "The date? It is December 21, 1945."

"I didn't ask for the date," he persistently replied. "I asked you for a date! You'd say yes if you knew how much trouble I had getting rid of all that popcorn so I'd have an excuse to come out here and talk to you. The girls wouldn't eat it fast enough so I spilled it on the floor."

She could feel her cheeks turning pink when she looked into his mocking eyes.

"I've been overseas for a couple years, but when I left fellows and girls did go out together." There was a decidedly impish gleam in his eyes when he asked, "Don't tell me that changed while I was gone!"

Straightening her shoulders and pulling herself to her full height of five-foot-seven inches, she returned his smile, but her voice sounded haughty to her own ears when she gave him her answer. "No. That hasn't changed, but I don't go out with people I don't know."

"You mean you would go out with me if we were properly introduced?" he asked.

"I...I..," she stammered. Then her voice took on a cutting edge when she asked, "What about your girlfriend?"

"You mean the girls I came in with?" he asked.

"Yes. It seems to me you've left your girlfriend and mother alone for too long," she said. "Don't you think it is time for you to go back to them?"

Her words apparently had a sobering effect on the young soldier who nodded curtly and muttered, "You may be right." With those words, he spun on his heels and determinedly strode away. June was surprised at the sense of disappointment she felt as she let her gaze follow his departing figure. Although she had made an effort to hide her feelings from him, she had enjoyed the give and take of their conversation.

As she busied herself with other customers, her thoughts returned to him, and she wondered why he had given up so easily. Before the evening was over, though, she would have the answer to that question.

Printed in the United States
140664LV00002B/4/P